W9-DFL-454

WHERE THERE'S A WILL…

Georges Feydeau

WHERE THERE'S A WILL…

(Le Système Ribadier)

in a new version by
Nicki Frei

OBERON BOOKS
LONDON

First published in this version in 2003 by Oberon Books Ltd.
(incorporating Absolute Classics)
521 Caledonian Road, London N7 9RH
Tel: 020 7607 3637 / Fax: 020 7607 3629

e-mail: oberon.books@btinternet.com

Copyright © adaptation Nicki Frei 2003

A catalogue record for this book is available from the British
Library.

ISBN: 1 84002 378 3

Cover illustration: Andrzej Klimowski

Printed in Great Britain by Antony Rowe Ltd, Chippenham.

Characters

SOPHIE
GUSMAN
ANGÈLE
RIBADIER
THOMMEREUX
SAVINET

Where There's A Will... was first performed at the Yvonne Arnaud Theatre, Guildford on 29 April 2003 with the following cast:

SOPHIE, Amanda Shillabeer

GUSMAN, Andrew Leonard

ANGÈLE, Elaine Paige

RIBADIER, Nicholas Le Prevost

THOMMEREUX, David Warner

SAVINET, David Bamber

Director, Peter Hall

ACT ONE

Scene 1

Paris 1895. An elegant first-floor reception room with French windows on to a balcony. Downstage, double doors lead to the hall. Two more doors, to right and left. Two sofas face one another across a large central pouf. Above the mantelpiece, a large full-length portrait of the late Robineau dominates the room.

SOPHIE, the maid, and GUSMAN, the groom, locked in tender farewells over the threshold of the open window. He disappears over the balcony, then reappears.

GUSMAN: One last little kiss, Sophie…

SOPHIE: Are you mad?

GUSMAN: Just a teeny-weeny one…

SOPHIE: All right then. Go on. But, be quick…

She offers him a spot on her neck. He scoops her up in a crushing embrace burying his face in her.

GUSMAN: Oh, Sophie!… I'd sooner have this… (*kissing her*) than all this…

He gestures round the opulent decor.

SOPHIE: Gusman! Not now. They'll be in any second. I've just served coffee. Stop it!

GUSMAN: We'll give them a thrill…

SOPHIE: And they'll give us the sack!

GUSMAN: When will I see you?

SOPHIE: Tonight, if you like…

GUSMAN: Tonight. Aren't they off out?

SOPHIE: (*shaking her head*) No. So, you're free… When it's all gone quiet, you can get in here – I'll leave it unlocked – and come up to my room… I shall expect the conduct of a gentleman, mind!

GUSMAN: Of course!

SOPHIE: They're coming! Get out!

She quickly shuts the window as he disappears.

Scene 2

ANGÈLE bursts in, a cup of coffee in hand.

ANGÈLE: All right! I heard you! Enough!

RIBADIER follows, also carrying a coffee cup.

RIBADIER: Enough! I want your word it will never happen again!

ANGÈLE: *You* want. *You* want.

RIBADIER: Yes, I do. (*noticing SOPHIE*) Leave us, Sophie.

He drinks his coffee.

SOPHIE: Yes, Monsieur. (*aside*) Unh, unh… Trouble!

SOPHIE exits.

RIBADIER: I think you've gone mad, really I do! Making a scene like that in front of the whole Committee!?! My wife!! I nearly died…

ANGÈLE: How else could I find out where you were?

She puts down her cup and goes to sit on a sofa.

RIBADIER: (*getting up*) How else?… I had *told* you: 'I am going to a meeting of the Transport Sub-Committee on Railways,' I said. Quite clear, to my mind. But, no, that's not enough for Madame who must come and check for herself. Pandemonium! Not five minutes after the Chairman has opened proceedings… And who's making this row? Madame, my wife, yelling: 'Where are these famous members? I want to see them for myself!'

A beat.

ANGÈLE: (*shrugging*) No one died or anything, did they?

RIBADIER: (*going to her*) You made a complete fool of yourself. And me.

ANGÈLE: Ah! *You!*

RIBADIER: Oh! You may not give a damn but I'm a man with a certain standing…a certain status… And I must insist such a thing never happens again. When I saw you there, honestly, I didn't know where to put myself. And as for the Chairman! The expression on his face! He let me have it once you'd gone: 'In future, Ribadier, it might be wise if you were to advise your wife that we meet in *private* session.' What could I say?

ANGÈLE: You flew to my defence?

RIBADIER: No! I grovelled. I said you'd been showing worrying signs of mental instability.

ANGÈLE: You said what?

RIBADIER: But the doctors anticipated a full recovery.

ANGÈLE: Charming!

RIBADIER: Well! What would you have said?

ANGÈLE: That I was a concerned wife… A woman who'd learned the hard way about the congenital infidelity of men! That's what I would've said!

RIBADIER: Here we go…

ANGÈLE: Committees: the unqualified discussing the unnecessary! I've never believed in them –

RIBADIER: But you've just been there! You've seen us all at it!

ANGÈLE: Well, of course, I saw *you*: the *men*... But you're politicians... You're organized, I know that. Breach of security. Plan B. Emergency measures...

RIBADIER: Oh, good Lord! Angèle!

ANGÈLE: Get the women out by a back door...

RIBADIER: I can assure you, my dear, that the members of the Government Transport Sub-Committee on Railways do not gather to play around with tarts!

ANGÈLE shrugs, clearly unconvinced.

You've no right to suspect me! When have I ever given you any reason to suppose I was unfaithful?

ANGÈLE: You? No, never... (*indicating the portrait*) But *him!*

RIBADIER: Ah, ah, ah, ah, ah, ah, aah! Him! Always him! Your Robineau! Is it my fault your first husband deceived you?

ANGÈLE: No. It's mine... But I was an innocent. So very young...

RIBADIER: Yes...

ANGÈLE: (*wagging a finger*) Not now. Those days are behind me.

RIBADIER: Yes...

She shoots him a dirty look.

ANGÈLE: The wretch! When I think how he cheated on me time and again... I never knew... Just look at him sneering down at me! (*to the portrait*) Scoundrel! Haven't you humiliated me enough?

RIBADIER: Go on! You let him have it!

ANGÈLE: (*to the portrait*) Taking advantage of your poor wife's trusting nature… (*to RIBADIER*) He had scores of mistresses right from the start!

RIBADIER: (*sympathetic*) Oh!

ANGÈLE: (*to the portrait*) Well, I'll have my revenge! I will take lovers!

RIBADIER: What?

ANGÈLE: (*to the portrait*) You'll know how it feels!

RIBADIER: Hey, hey, hey, hey! Angèle! Calm down! There's been a change of personnel, remember? (*indicating the portrait*) Number one is history. And he's dead.

ANGÈLE: Ah, so he is… I get so furious!

RIBADIER: Quite crazed! I know! I'm the one who gets it in the neck! *He* was a degenerate goat! I'm not! You've got to…move on!

ANGÈLE: It's the portrait. Every time I see it, my blood boils…

RIBADIER: Have it put in the attic. Simple. Why keep it out?

He sits down by the table.

ANGÈLE: Not on his account. But it's a Manet. You don't put a Manet in the attic. Even one of him. And he is rather…decorative.

RIBADIER: (*piqued*) That's as maybe… But must we live in his toxic thrall?… Perhaps I should have it updated… A few touches would do it. A little less here… (*indicating hairline*) A little more there. (*indicating a paunch*) Time does for us all in the end… It might help –

ANGÈLE: – No. I want to keep him, it, as it is.

RIBADIER: Ah!

ANGÈLE: I like having this nonpareil of conjugal infidelity under my nose! It reminds me not to trust you.

RIBADIER: Me? Good God, why me?

ANGÈLE: Because you're my husband.

RIBADIER: That's the reason?

ANGÈLE: It's the best. This portrait says: 'Never forget: all husbands are liars and cheats.' It's not personal, you understand, just a fact of life.

RIBADIER: So sayeth Robineau, eh? A tablet of stone from on high.

ANGÈLE: Quite. 'BEWARE!!' he adds. 'Take heed. All your husbands will betray you just as I did.'

RIBADIER: *All* your husbands?

ANGÈLE: 'Don't trust in appearances. The blacker his sins, the better the cover up… Maintain surveillance at all times: peek, pry, probe… If you find nothing, you haven't looked hard enough! Search again: there's always something to hide!'

RIBADIER: This'll make you run mad!

ANGÈLE: That's Robineau's message. Courtesy of Manet…

RIBADIER: I'll have it burnt! I'll throw it in the fire.

Furious, he makes for the painting.

ANGÈLE: (*taking RIBADIER's arm, restrains him*) I was made a fool of once… It won't happen again. Not if I can help it.

RIBADIER: Good God! Honestly! Can't you see?… It's totally irrational! Just because Robineau –

ANGÈLE: – Robineau's out of the picture. (*pleased at the thought*) He's meeting his Maker… Judgement Day!

RIBADIER: Poor old Robineau!

ANGÈLE: He's gone. You are still here. And I've learnt my lesson. That's why, when I married you, I made myself one promise: you were sweet and trusting with Robineau… (*crossing herself*) You'll be tough and suspicious with Ribadier… (*crosses herself again*)

RIBADIER: Excuse me! What's this…? (*crossing himself*)

ANGÈLE: No. Sorry. Mistake.

RIBADIER: A tad premature, my dear! Really! Sizing up the coffin –

ANGÈLE: – Watch me nail down the lid if I ever catch you out!

RIBADIER: When? How? You dog my footsteps; you follow me everywhere…

ANGÈLE: Indeed, I do. And I know all your tricks and dodges…

RIBADIER: Oh, really?

ANGÈLE: Every one of them. I have the complete anthology!

She brandishes a small leather-bound notebook.

RIBADIER: What's that?

ANGÈLE: A full catalogue of my first husband's escapades.

13

RIBADIER: What?

ANGÈLE: When he was alive…

RIBADIER: Of course…

ANGÈLE: The bastard! Doing it wasn't enough, he had to write it all down!… To enlighten posterity, no doubt! Adulterer and archivist! That's how I know about it.

RIBADIER: How unbelievably stupid! You may do these things… All right. But you don't keep a record!

ANGÈLE: That's your moral position, is it? Do it but don't write about it.

RIBADIER: Yes! No!

ANGÈLE: He made quite a job of it. There's footnotes, an index… And a title even…

RIBADIER: Really?

ANGÈLE: (*with a hollow chuckle*) Yes. 'Emergency Lifesavers'!

RIBADIER: 'Emergency Lifesavers'?!

ANGÈLE: Sub-title: '365 Practical Solutions for Unimaginative Husbands.'

RIBADIER: Good Lord! That's a new one for every day of the year.

ANGÈLE: Quite.

RIBADIER: That's not an emergency; it's a permanent crisis!

ANGÈLE: Anyway, I know all the tricks now. You can't fool me: I have the manual!

RIBADIER: Oh, really! Don't be absurd!

RIBADIER snatches the book and leafs through it.

These are the ramblings of a shameless egotist, not some cosmic creed…

RIBADIER scornfully tosses the book on to a sofa.

ANGÈLE: Rant all you like… I'll find you out, d'you hear… (*picking up the book*) I'd rather know the bitter truth than live with this maddening doubt…

RIBADIER: (*furious*) Oh!

ANGÈLE: (*leaving*) I'll find you out!

ANGÈLE exits.

Scene 3

RIBADIER: (*alone*) Oh!… And I only married her because I wanted an amenable wife! (*to the portrait*) It's all your fault: boasting how sweet and credulous she was… Never any 'Where are you going?' or 'Where have you been?'… Just look at her now! What a life! Every move, every look, every breath monitored… It's intolerable!… And it's cramping my style…

ANGÈLE enters.

Ooops! It's her.

Scene 4

RIBADIER: Back again?

ANGÈLE hesitates a moment before going over to him.

ANGÈLE: Eugène, I was wrong. I apologize!

RIBADIER: Why bother? You'll be off again in five minutes. Like a child.

ANGÈLE: No, really I won't. I'm serious.

RIBADIER: You say that every time.

ANGÈLE: Yes, but I've never really meant it. I do now…

RIBADIER: Now, perhaps, but not for long… (*softening*) Oh, all right… Come here.

He kisses her.

ANGÈLE: I'm a reformed woman! Here: these are for you. (*hands him some letters*) I haven't even read them.

RIBADIER: How nice of you! What have we here? Good Lord! They're addressed to me at the Club! How did you get them?

ANGÈLE: I went to pick them up.

RIBADIER: I beg your pardon!

ANGÈLE: I told the footman: 'My husband has asked that I should collect his post.' And he handed them over.

RIBADIER: Oh, really! My private correspondence! How dare he hand it over to just anyone…

ANGÈLE: 'Just anyone'. Charming. May a wife not collect her husband's post?

RIBADIER: No!

ANGÈLE: I didn't even take a peek…

RIBADIER: Oh, my God!

ANGÈLE: You go on about me spying on you… (*indicating the letters*) Well? Not true, eh? (*off his reaction*) Why don't you read them?

RIBADIER: What?

ANGÈLE: Your letters.

RIBADIER: I will. Later.

ANGÈLE: 'Later'. When I'm not here… Perhaps there's something you don't want me to see?

RIBADIER: Oh, God, you are driving me mad! (*quickly scanning the envelopes*) Look at you! You've only just apologized! (*offering them to her*) Anyway, go on, read them! I've nothing to hide.

ANGÈLE leafs through the envelopes and immediately discards the first four.

ANGÈLE: Ah. Bill... Bill... Circular... Bill...

RIBADIER: (*all injured innocence*) There! What did you think you'd find?

ANGÈLE: (*examining the last letter*) Ah! Now this is more promising... Good weight. A more elegant hand... (*turning over the envelope*) A deckled edge... Oh, and a motto.

RIBADIER: (*alarmed*) A motto? Really? Good God!

ANGÈLE: (*reads salaciously*) '*Salus populi suprema est lex!*'

A beat.

RIBADIER: (*relieved*) It's Latin!

ANGÈLE: Quite! But what's it mean?

RIBADIER: Ah, well, now... Let's see. (*taking the letter*) '*Salus populi suprema est lex!*' '*Est*', 'is'...obviously. '*Salus*', salute, greetings... Ho, ho. Yes, I see... Very good. Loses in the translation somewhat, darling –

ANGÈLE, bored, grabs the letter back and rips it open.

(*snatching it back*) Hey!

RIBADIER takes his time extracting the letter and smoothing the page before reading.

'Dear Sir, As a committed Republican, you'll endorse the sentiments expressed in our new motto...' Well, yes, of course... Cicero, apparently. I thought so... Blah! Blah!

Blah! New motto; new letterhead; get your order in now... That's all...

He thrusts the letter into ANGÈLE's hands.

(*loftily*) Now, if there's nothing else to keep me from my work...

ANGÈLE: Well, how was I to know it was some political slogan? You should write them in a language people understand! What *does* it mean? –

RIBADIER: – This is typical! You lash out with wild accusations, then find they're completely unfounded. It's insulting! It's intolerable! Keep it up and I'll be off!

ANGÈLE: You'd leave me?

RIBADIER: Certainly! I have family. I'll go back to my mother!

ANGÈLE: You wouldn't.

RIBADIER: I would.

ANGÈLE: Eugène! Eugène, I do apologize.

RIBADIER: Again!

ANGÈLE: It was very wrong of me to suspect you.

RIBADIER: (*like a sulky child*) Yes, it was...

ANGÈLE: I shouldn't have accused you like that.

RIBADIER: Quite.

ANGÈLE: I wouldn't be like this if it weren't for Robineau and his horrid book...

RIBADIER: 'Emergency Lifesavers'? (*a smug laugh*) Honestly, darling... If I did intend to deceive you, d'you think I'd resort to his tired old tricks? No! Give me credit, at least, for originality. I'm an educated man. I can do my own creative thinking...

ANGÈLE: I'd rather you didn't...

RIBADIER: Well... Take care. Don't push me too far. A crushed and tormented man will look around for refuge...

ANGÈLE: Oh! Oh!

RIBADIER: Inevitably...

ANGÈLE: Oh, come on, Eugène. It's not all my fault. I wouldn't get so worked up if I thought you really loved me.

RIBADIER: I don't love you!

ANGÈLE: Not like you used to. A woman can always tell. One day you barely speak to me...

RIBADIER: Oh!

ANGÈLE: The next you tell me everything twice. No, you don't love me that much any more...

RIBADIER: I do, I do! But these constant rows; they rob a relationship of its romance. A man starts the day with a finite store of emotional energy. You make a scene, I get angry, we quarrel... Pouf! It's gone! I have to refuel...

ANGÈLE: I must have more reserves...

RIBADIER: You're a woman! I'm like a man on a budget: if he fritters money on snacks, he can't buy himself dinner...

ANGÈLE: Unless someone treats him to a free meal.

RIBADIER: Ah! You said it!

ANGÈLE stamps her foot and bursts into tears.

ANGÈLE: But I don't want you dining out. I want you at home, feasting with me!

RIBADIER: There, there. Yes, of course. (*coaxing*) Only you mustn't spoil my appetite…

ANGÈLE: And you mustn't eat between meals…

She hugs him impulsively. He returns the embrace.

RIBADIER: And we won't ever start again…

ANGÈLE: I promise!

RIBADIER: (*aside*) You think that's an end to it? Not a hope!

Scene 5

RIBADIER and ANGÈLE leap apart as SOPHIE enters.

RIBADIER: Ah, Sophie! What is it?

SOPHIE: Nothing, Monsieur.

RIBADIER: Ah, good.

ANGÈLE: What do you want, Sophie?

SOPHIE: There's a telegram for Monsieur, Madame.

ANGÈLE: Well, give it to him!

SOPHIE: But Madame told me to –

ANGÈLE: – Yes, yes… I've changed my mind.

ANGÈLE exits.

Scene 6

RIBADIER: So, Sophie, what is it?

SOPHIE: It's, it's a telegram for Monsieur.

RIBADIER: (*taking it; anxious*) For me! A telegram! (*reading*) Oh! Some crisis in the Senate… Nothing important.

(*aside*) Ouf! That was scary.

(*to SOPHIE*) How is it, Mademoiselle, that you deliver telegrams to Madame that are addressed to me?

SOPHIE: She slipped me twenty francs.

RIBADIER: What!?! I'm shocked! In my own house! It's shameful! Aren't you ashamed?… Look, here's thirty…

SOPHIE: Huh?

RIBADIER: Give Madame back her twenty… And in future, you'll give everything to me…preferably when I'm alone…

SOPHIE: Ah, ha! Very well.

RIBADIER: Good. Off you go!

SOPHIE makes to leave, then turns and retraces her steps.

SOPHIE: For forty francs, Monsieur, I'd give you Madame's letters too.

RIBADIER: What? Really? You'd deliver –

Doorbell.

Doorbell! Good! Go and answer it.

SOPHIE: Yes, Monsieur.

SOPHIE walks to door.

RIBADIER: If it's for me, ask them to wait; I've a telegram to write. Go!

She exits.

(*aside*) Thank God I rumbled this little plot in time. Lord knows what might have fallen into her hands…

He exits.

21

Scene 7

SOPHIE: This way, Monsieur.

THOMMEREUX: God! What emotional turmoil!… They say absence makes the heart grow fonder! How true! (*to SOPHIE*) Go! Inform your Mistress!

SOPHIE: What name shall I give?

THOMMEREUX: Aristide Thommereux!… No! A little more mystery… Say it's a friend, back from the Orient!

SOPHIE: The Orient. That's some way off, is it, Monsieur?

THOMMEREUX shrugs carelessly and deposits his hat and cane. SOPHIE heads for the door.

THOMMEREUX: Tell me, my girl. Is it true, the news I've heard?

SOPHIE: Depends what it is.

THOMMEREUX: That poor Robineau is…no longer with us?

SOPHIE: Monsieur Robineau? He went two years ago!

THOMMEREUX: Yes. And they say time's a great healer… But, my poor friend, two whole years later… I weep still…

SOPHIE: Perhaps you haven't known for long?

THOMMEREUX: Quarter of an hour! Straight from the train, I ran to their old house… There, they told me of the loss of my friend, my dear friend… I loved him like a brother… I asked for the widow's address and here I am! It's been quite a blow for me…

SOPHIE: (*a sympathetic sigh*) Ah!

THOMMEREUX: (*sighing too*) Ah!… And here?

SOPHIE: Here? Oh, well, we're used to it here.

THOMMEREUX: (*noticing the portrait*) And there he is! Just as I remember him! Well, a little flattered maybe… But still him!

SOPHIE: I'll inform Madame.

THOMMEREUX: Yes, off you go.

Scene 8

THOMMEREUX: (*addressing the portrait*) My poor friend… Now I can marry your wife! Assume your rôle… Oh, I could have elbowed you out long ago… Before… But I chose to banish myself rather than betray a friend whom I loved like a brother… And I did love you with all my heart. You did me a good turn, the best, the sort that forges a life-long bond. I was going to marry – a charming woman who'd proposed to me herself… You came and said: 'Don't marry her! Instinct tells me you'll regret it!' I took your advice… Three months later, she had a baby… She hadn't loved me at all! You saved me and I've always been profoundly grateful. From that day on, we were like this…

THOMMEREUX locks his fingers together.

'What's mine is yours,' you said, 'except my wife!' (*aside*) Why just his wife? (*shrugs*) It was a pact; I was bound… (*to the portrait*) Alas, I can confess it to you now: I fell – I don't know how – instantly, madly, perversely in love with Angèle… One sultry afternoon, she had a silk scarf draped round her neck. 'Please,' she said, 'Take this wretched thing off me.' I turned to oblige her…all courtesy…not really thinking… But there was her neck…pale skin, blond tendrils of hair. I was entranced by this graceful swan-like vision… My lips brushed her skin in a tiny, involuntary kiss…

A beat.

Then, Angèle's voice cut across the dream: 'Oh, we shouldn't… We shouldn't be doing this…' Alarm bells! Somehow I pulled back from the precipice… My heart was thumping wildly… I popped a pill: I needed to think – coolly and rationally… The next day, I took up a diplomatic post in the Far East. That's what I did for you… Because I loved you like a brother… I left without looking back… I was your friend: loyal and true! Seduce your wife? Betray my brother? Never! It's not in my nature!

A beat.

I didn't despair completely. 'Robineau took a young bride,' I said to myself, 'He'll die in the saddle… Then you can reappear and marry his wife with a clear conscience. You won't have stolen her, merely inherited her…and that happens in the best families.' I waited. You went. Here I am!

ANGÈLE enters.

ANGÈLE: Back from the Orient? Who can it be?

THOMMEREUX: Angèle!

ANGÈLE: You!

THOMMEREUX: Ah, Angèle! What joy to see you again!

ANGÈLE: Whatever happened to you?

THOMMEREUX: Voluntary exile overseas… Because
    I was in love with you…

ANGÈLE: Stop it!

THOMMEREUX: And I couldn't tell you… Oh, Angèle!
    Life!… We strut our hour upon the stage…

ANGÈLE: What?

THOMMEREUX: The trials we must endure…

ANGÈLE watches in surprise as THOMMEREUX points sombrely at the portrait.

There he is, my dear friend! I loved him like a brother. And you, his poor, grieving widow, preserving his image like a shrine.

ANGÈLE: Robineau!?! Ha! A nice fellow he turned out to be…

THOMMEREUX: What?

ANGÈLE: You thought he was the model husband. You believed, like me, that he was loving and faithful –

THOMMEREUX: – No! Really?

ANGÈLE: Yes! Not once but hundreds of times. There! That's something to weep over.

THOMMEREUX: Angèle, I am pained, of course I am… But I'm also thrilled to bits!

ANGÈLE: Why?

THOMMEREUX: Because I won't suffer in his memory. Any comparisons you draw between us must favour me!

ANGÈLE: (*nonplussed*) What are you talking about?

THOMMEREUX: The impediment impedes no longer!

ANGÈLE is still in the dark.

He's dead; I love you; let's get married.

ANGÈLE: Us!?! (*bursts out laughing*) Oh, my poor dear friend…

THOMMEREUX: What's the matter?

ANGÈLE: You! Marry you!… There's just one little problem.

THOMMEREUX: Nothing I can't handle!

ANGÈLE: My husband!

THOMMEREUX: What?

ANGÈLE: I remarried. I'm sorry.

A beat.

THOMMEREUX: It's a test, isn't it? You'd never do that.

ANGÈLE: I've done it.

THOMMEREUX: I don't believe it.

RIBADIER's voice off-stage.

ANGÈLE: My husband. You can ask him yourself.

Scene 9

RIBADIER: (*aside*) I wonder who's here…

THOMMEREUX: Ribadier!

RIBADIER: Thommereux! You're here, in Paris!

THOMMEREUX: It's Ribadier!

RIBADIER: Are you all right?

THOMMEREUX: Fine!… And you? Have you been keeping well since I last saw you?

RIBADIER: Last saw you! It's been three years! Did you know I'd got married? This is my wife. Let me introduce you –

ANGÈLE: – No need. We know each other… Slightly… (*glances at the portrait*) From before…

RIBADIER: Oh! Under the previous regime!

THOMMEREUX: (*emotional*) Yes. In poor Robineau's day… There he is, my dear, dear friend. Dead!… (*shaking his head*) He was always so lively! Vigorous, vital, vivacious, virile…

RIBADIER / ANGÈLE: (*embarrassed*) Yes. Yes, indeed…

THOMMEREUX: Va, va, vroom by the bucket load! (*aside*) Not striking the right note here, I can tell.

RIBADIER: And you're back to stay? No more flights to the Far East?

THOMMEREUX: Oh, yes!

RIBADIER: Yes!?! Good Lord, why?

THOMMEREUX: (*pointedly*) Arriving here, I suffered so crushing a disappointment, that the best thing is for me simply to disappear again.

RIBADIER: Oh, come along now! What disappointment? A woman, no doubt! Some faithless tart who's forgotten you?

THOMMEREUX: There was never anything between us.

RIBADIER: So you've lost nothing! Terrific! Be patient! Your turn will come, I promise…

THOMMEREUX: It's not up to you.

RIBADIER: Pity. You'd be fixed up already!

THOMMEREUX: Brave fellow!

ANGÈLE: (*aside*) Oh, la, la…

RIBADIER: Meanwhile, we're going to hang on to you. Where are your bags?

THOMMEREUX: My bags? Back at the Hôtel de France where I left them.

RIBADIER: Right! I'll have them picked up and brought over here.

THOMMEREUX / ANGÈLE: Huh?

RIBADIER: We've a whole summerhouse at your disposal in the garden.

THOMMEREUX: But I couldn't possibly…

RIBADIER: Of course, you could.

ANGÈLE: (*aside*) Have him here? He's mad! (*aloud*) But, darling, the summerhouse isn't really habitable…

RIBADIER: Yes, it is! Well, habitable enough for him! (*to THOMMEREUX*) Actually it's full of cockroaches.

THOMMEREUX: Ah!

RIBADIER: That's why I don't rent it out. It wouldn't do for strangers; but it's perfect for a friend! You don't mind, do you? The odd paltry Parisian cockroach won't bother a man who's tangled with all the creepy crawlies of the East.

THOMMEREUX: Ha, ha. Yes. Out there, the cockroaches are scorpions.

RIBADIER / ANGÈLE: Scorpions!

THOMMEREUX: Some a foot long, if you please!

RIBADIER: There you are! This man has slept among foot-long scorpions. Can you imagine?

ANGÈLE: Euh! Horrible!

RIBADIER: He'll think himself well off with the wild life in our summerhouse.

THOMMEREUX: No, really, it's too much of an imposition…

RIBADIER: No, really, it's not. I can't rent the place out in that state, so I'm more than willing to let you have it. Come on. I'll have it made ready.

THOMMEREUX: Really, Eugène…

RIBADIER: No trouble. No trouble at all.

RIBADIER exits.

Scene 10

THOMMEREUX: I really can't accept his offer.

ANGÈLE: No. I beg you not to.

THOMMEREUX: Why?

ANGÈLE: After all you said to me earlier… After that cryptic confession in front of my husband… After all that's happened between us!

THOMMEREUX: But nothing has happened between us! Ever!

ANGÈLE: Precisely! If something had gone on, well what's done is done and we'd have to live with it… But nothing did: we emerged unscathed from our moment of weakness… I'm referring to that sultry afternoon…

THOMMEREUX: I remember it well.

ANGÈLE: Ah, me too… A woman is full of contradictions… I loved Robineau… But, then, for one wild moment… Fortunately, at that critical point, you pulled back, downed tools and withdrew…

THOMMEREUX: I loved Robineau like a brother!

ANGÈLE: Your scruples saved me!

THOMMEREUX: Oh, God!!!

ANGÈLE: Anyway, we can't possibly live in the same house. Seeing each other every day would be embarrassing for me and agonising for you.

THOMMEREUX: I see. Because *you* married Ribadier
without waiting for me when you knew I loved you,
I must withdraw and cast myself into exile…

ANGÈLE: It's for your own good.

THOMMEREUX: Ribadier's good, you mean… Still,
I suppose you must love him as you married him.

ANGÈLE: It wasn't that so much…

THOMMEREUX: Then why did you do it?

ANGÈLE: I couldn't remain a widow… It's too awkward…
So, after a decorous interlude…when Ribadier seemed
smitten…

THOMMEREUX: (*a bitter laugh*) Ah!

ANGÈLE: Then there was his name: 'Ribadier'.

THOMMEREUX: You liked his name!

ANGÈLE: It weighed in the balance… Robineau,
Ribadier… Same initial… No need to change all the
linen and silver.

THOMMEREUX is still in the dark.

The monogram…

THOMMEREUX: I see! A marriage of thrift! I've heard of
love-matches and marriages of convenience but never,
ever one of good housekeeping! If you'd wed him for his
fine moustache or his elegant clothes, I could understand
it… But marrying to save a bit of needlework on the odd
pillowcase!…

ANGÈLE: Sheets, too. And towels, tablecloths, napkins,
handkerchiefs, laundry bags –

THOMMEREUX: – No! No, it's quite beyond me!

ANGÈLE: All right. Calm down.

THOMMEREUX: I'd have paid a seamstress good money to see that 'R' removed.

ANGÈLE: Oh, well! I do love him now... So it's all turned out for the best.

THOMMEREUX: You do love him! Oh, tell me straight! Don't spare my feelings. Rub salt in the wound, why don't you?

ANGÈLE: You see now why you must go.

THOMMEREUX: You're right. I only arrived today from the Far East. Still, I shall return...

ANGÈLE: When?

THOMMEREUX: Tomorrow morning.

ANGÈLE: Good.

THOMMEREUX: Quite a round-trip for one fruitless night in Paris!

ANGÈLE: Invent some excuse for my husband to explain why you're going... And so, farewell, my friend, farewell forever.

ANGÈLE heads for the door.

THOMMEREUX: Farewell forever! (*calling her back*) Angèle, just promise me one thing: no one's immortal... Ribadier, say, or me even...we could just pop off one day...

ANGÈLE: Oh!

THOMMEREUX: If ever such misfortune should strike him – or me – either of us – or both... Promise that you'll write immediately: 'Come! I am free!'

ANGÈLE: Stop it. Don't talk about such things.

THOMMEREUX: Yes, but...do I have your word?

ANGÈLE: Farewell!

ANGÈLE exits.

Scene 11

THOMMEREUX: (*alone*) Farewell! How final that sounds! But she's right; I must go straight back to Saigon and my scorpions! I've nothing to hope for here.

RIBADIER enters.

RIBADIER: Where's my wife?

THOMMEREUX: She just left.

RIBADIER: Oh, well... I've told them to get the summerhouse ready for you.

THOMMEREUX: No. I can't... It's all hopeless... Let me take my leave!

RIBADIER: What? I thought we were agreed!... Bit of a gloomy bugger, aren't you?

THOMMEREUX: What d'you expect?

RIBADIER: Right! Well, we'll have to cheer you up.

THOMMEREUX: Nothing can cheer me up any more.

RIBADIER: How can you say that? You're in gay Paris!

THOMMEREUX: I hate Paris.

RIBADIER: I'm good company, aren't I?

THOMMEREUX: Yes, but –

RIBADIER: – And my wife is charming?

THOMMEREUX: Perfectly! That's my problem!

RIBADIER: What?

THOMMEREUX: (*recovering himself*) Er… That Paris has so little allure for me. Most people love it. *That's* my problem! (*aside*) Good Lord! I forgot he was her husband!

THOMMEREUX retrieves his hat and cane.

I've told you that I wish to leave… I'm going back to the Far East.

RIBADIER: (*relieving him of hat and cane*) Good God, man, now you're getting on my nerves! You're staying here! I won't let any man behave so foolishly over a woman!

RIBADIER deposits THOMMEREUX's things upstage on the windowseat.

All this wailing and wringing of hands won't win her back. Wrong tactic! Get back on the offensive! She won't come looking if you're skulking in a corner.

THOMMEREUX: She won't come looking. Full stop.

RIBADIER: Really, my friend, you know nothing about women. Would you like me to sort her out for you? Just to show you how it's done, I mean… Observe my method: watch me broach the lady, study her, feel my way, probe her –

THOMMEREUX: (*all lofty indignation*) – 'Probe her?'… Oh, please don't. What a ghastly expression!

RIBADIER: Get the feel of her. Explore the lie of the land. What did you think I meant?… I'll find the chink in her armour and show you the way to beat her drum!

THOMMEREUX: Stop it!… Oh, stop it now!

RIBADIER: You don't trust me, do you… You're afraid I'd pinch the woman of your dreams…

THOMMEREUX: Me! You! Oh…

RIBADIER: I don't make a habit of it, I assure you. All right, I did step into your shoes at Mimi Marjolin's six years ago… But, then, Mimi was always a bit of a slapper…

THOMMEREUX: It was you! She dropped me for *you!*

RIBADIER: Didn't you know?

THOMMEREUX: She never told me.

RIBADIER: Oh, I thought…

THOMMEREUX: I have to say, I'm quite offended!

RIBADIER: Why? You split up six years ago!

THOMMEREUX: I find it most disagreeable. How would you feel if you'd drunk a good glass of claret and someone said: 'Ah, well, now I can tell you that the waiter spat in it beforehand.' It leaves a nasty taste in the mouth. Quite disgusting!

RIBADIER: Thank you for that kind analogy!

THOMMEREUX: I didn't mean to say… (*aside*) You stuck your spoon in my soup! Oh, how I'd like to –

RIBADIER: – So, we're agreed. You'll let me approach this lady on your behalf.

THOMMEREUX: Are you mad? You're married to her! (*recovering frantically*) Your wife, I mean! You're married to your wife… And she's quite charming!

RIBADIER: Napoleon dictated to two secretaries at once.

THOMMEREUX: You are not Napoleon! Oh, really… (*aside*) Typical politician! Only really wants to talk about himself! (*aloud*) What about Madame Ribadier? Doesn't she get jealous?

RIBADIER: Jealous! Her! Saints alive! You should hear her!... She's a lovely woman but sometimes she makes my life a living hell!

THOMMEREUX: You're not happy then?

RIBADIER: Not always...

THOMMEREUX: (*aside*) Not happy!... He's not happy! It's true what they say: one man profits from another's misfortune...

RIBADIER: And she used to be so trusting...so gullible... Well, you knew them; Robineau must have told you.

THOMMEREUX: Often.

RIBADIER: Lord knows why he had to flaunt his infidelities at her! (*off his reaction*) Well, he didn't... Not exactly. But he allowed her to find out. D'you know what he did, that confounded idiot –

THOMMEREUX: – don't call him an idiot! I loved him like a brother!

RIBADIER: Fair enough!... Your 'brother' left amongst his papers a sort of inventory of all the ploys he'd used to deceive his wife.

THOMMEREUX: So?

RIBADIER: So! Unfortunate epiphany for Angèle! Scales gone! And not just as far as Robineau was concerned. No! All husbands in general!... What's worse, if ever she did catch me out – I know her, she's a vindictive woman – she'd never forgive me!

THOMMEREUX: Dear, dear.

RIBADIER: She'd have her revenge. She'd really put the screws on...

THOMMEREUX: (*smothering a laugh*) Yes. Well, better not deceive her then!

RIBADIER: Oh, I wouldn't go that far… But I have to take extra precautions. Actually, I've got a little flirtation going right now.

THOMMEREUX: (*aside*) Oh, goody!

RIBADIER: The wife of a wine merchant. A charming brunette.

THOMMEREUX: How will you slip her surveillance now your wife knows all the tricks?

RIBADIER: I won't slip her surveillance, I'll 'suspend' it.

THOMMEREUX: How?

RIBADIER: Where there's a will, Thommereux…

THOMMEREUX: Yes?

RIBADIER: I have my own cunning device; nothing like those crude ploys Robineau came up with… His methods were amateurish; *mine* operate in the realm of science.

A beat as THOMMEREUX grapples with this idea.

THOMMEREUX: No. Don't understand.

RIBADIER: May I invite you to my next demonstration?

THOMMEREUX: Oh, please do.

RIBADIER: You'll have to stay here. You can't go straight back to Saigon.

THOMMEREUX: I realise that.

RIBADIER: Good.

THOMMEREUX: (*aside*) Yes, I'll stay… Angèle can't blame me; it's her husband who insisted…

Scene 12

SOPHIE enters.

SOPHIE: The summerhouse is ready.

RIBADIER: (*to THOMMEREUX*) Good. Would you like to see your rooms?

THOMMEREUX: Yes, indeed… And I can freshen up a little.

RIBADIER: Sophie will show you the way.

SOPHIE: Yes, Monsieur.

SOPHIE hands RIBADIER a telegram.

This telegram's just arrived for Monsieur.

RIBADIER: Thank you.

SOPHIE: Monsieur will notice that I gave it straight to him.

RIBADIER: If you say so, Sophie…

SOPHIE: (*to THOMMEREUX*) This way, if you please, Monsieur.

THOMMEREUX: See you later.

RIBADIER: Yes.

SOPHIE and THOMMEREUX exit.

Scene 13

RIBADIER: (*opening the telegram*) Thérèse Savinet! It's from her! God, if this had fallen into my wife's hands. Hmm. One of life's close shaves. (*reading*) 'Bébé!' (*smiling*) 'Bébé.' That's me! 'Bébé, my husband has been called away suddenly to see a vineyard in Bourgogne. So I'm free this evening and I've given the servants the night off. I'll expect you at nine o'clock.' (*looking at his watch*) Good Lord! Nine o'clock! It's half past eight! I haven't a moment to lose. (*seeing ANGÈLE enter*) My wife! Bang on cue! I'll only just have time…

ANGÈLE carries a work basket which she places on a table.

ANGÈLE: Has your friend gone?

RIBADIER: He's in the summerhouse. Hey, hey… Why won't you look at me? Are you still cross with me?

ANGÈLE: Me? No! I know you don't cheat on me.

RIBADIER: Well, then, look me straight in the eye. There. Your hands in mine. (*takes her hands*) Do I look like an unfaithful husband? Could I look at you like this if I were deceiving you? Don't you see in my eyes how much I love you?

ANGÈLE eyes glaze over and she falls back on to the sofa.

ANGÈLE: Is it true?… You love me?…

RIBADIER: Yes. I love you. (*seeing ANGÈLE asleep*) There we go! (*smugly, to the audience*) Hypnosis: The Ribadier Method! (*to the portrait*) That one's not in your book, old man!

Scene 14

THOMMEREUX enters.

THOMMEREUX: Ah, dear fellow, I shall be fine out there.

RIBADIER: Jolly good. (*getting his hat*) I'm going out. Are you coming?

THOMMEREUX: Me? I… (*noticing ANGÈLE asleep*) My God! Angèle's asleep… Madame. Your wife.

RIBADIER: Leave her to it.

THOMMEREUX: But, look… What's wrong with her?

RIBADIER: Nothing! She's a work in progress. Demonstrable proof of the efficacy of the Ribadier Method!

THOMMEREUX: Huh?

RIBADIER: Hypnosis! She'll sleep like a horse while I'm out. When I get back, I'll blow on her hands and… (*snaps his fingers*) She'll wake up none the wiser.

RIBADIER goes to lock the doors.

THOMMEREUX: (*aside*) Oh, the wretch! (*to RIBADIER*) Now what are you up to?

RIBADIER: Locking the doors… You know, the servants. And I dim the lights so as not to attract attention from the street.

He lowers the lights. We see a bold bright moon.

Right. Let's go.

THOMMEREUX: Well, well…

RIBADIER waits for him on the threshold.

What? You're going to lock that one too?

RIBADIER: Of course, I am.

THOMMEREUX: (*aside*) What a devil! (*suddenly*) Ah, ha!

THOMMEREUX runs to the window and fumbles with the handle.

RIBADIER: What are you doing?

THOMMEREUX: I'm just getting my cane; you left it here.

THOMMEREUX manages to pick up the cane and leave the French window slightly ajar.

RIBADIER: Right! Ready now?

THOMMEREUX: I'm coming… (*aside*) But I'll be back! Well, he's really only an acquaintance. I've never loved *him* like a brother!

They exit. The sound of a key turning in the lock. Curtain.

End of Act One.

ACT TWO

Scene 1

ANGÈLE is still asleep in the dim room. At the window, illuminated by the moonlight, a silhouette appears climbing lithely up to the balcony. Outside the balustrade still, GUSMAN leans across and pushes against the French window which opens easily.

GUSMAN: Sophie didn't forget! I knew she wouldn't. Lust pricked her on… Right! Leg over!

GUSMAN throws a leg over the balustrade. Swivelling round to bring over the second leg, something catches on the wrought iron.

Oh, hang on, I'm caught…

Impatiently he pulls away; the sound of material being torn.

I've torn it. Oh, well, all in a good cause…

GUSMAN enters, looking and feeling for the tear but he can't find it in the gloom.

It's bloody dark in here. Ah! The lamp's not quite out…

He steps carefully towards the lamp and falls over ANGÈLE asleep in the armchair. She doesn't stir. GUSMAN feels his way round her prone figure.

Hell!… What is it? Something warm… Breathing!… Oh, it's the dog…slipped in here somehow… (*stroking and patting*) Naughty girl! There, there. Sssh! Good dog…

GUSMAN creeps on tiptoe to the door.

Phew! Lucky the bitch didn't bite me…bumping into her like that…

GUSMAN tries the door: it's locked. Incredulous, he rattles the handle and slaps the door with the flat of his hand. ANGÈLE stirs. GUSMAN whips round in alarm.

Stay. Stay. Good girl! (*very frustrated*) Aaargh!

GUSMAN paces a moment in thought: a solution strikes him.

Ah, the drainpipe!

(*making his way back to the window*) Good thing Sophie's room's at the back...

(*on the balcony; looking up*) Light's on. Right, here goes...

GUSMAN starts his climb. The stage remains still for a moment. Then, at the window, another silhouette appears also making the ascent to the first floor. Unlike GUSMAN, THOMMEREUX is clearly finding the climb quite a struggle. Much puffing and grunting. He finally makes it to the far side of the balustrade where he stops to catch his breath.

THOMMEREUX: Good Lord! The window's wide open. I only left it ajar. Wind, I suppose... Well, whatever, the game's afoot and time is short!

THOMMEREUX makes to jump the balustrade but falls back on the same side. He clutches at his heart.

Ouf! My heart! It's knocking against my ribs...bursting with passion!... Well, I hope that's what it is... Right, come along! *Courage!* One last push...

The clock rings nine.

Nine o'clock! The hour between the lap-dog and the wolf... Better get on with it, Thommereux!

He clambers over the balustrade with some difficulty.

Ouf! There we are!... I'm quite the Romeo – scaling walls, climbing through windows... Nothing above the first floor... That's quite high enough. Even Romeo might have thought twice if Juliet's balcony had been five floors up.

THOMMEREUX turns up the lamp and carries it over to the sofa. He stands contemplating ANGÈLE for a moment.

Oh, if Ribadier could see me now… Actually, I'd rather he didn't…because – and there's no getting round this – I am behaving in the most despicable manner. It's not on, you know, to cuckold a man when living under his roof… Still, it happens… She's so beautiful! Look at her! As exquisite as any Michaelangelo Madonna… I should deny myself… No… No… I can't. No bonds of friendship can restrain me…

THOMMEREUX puts the lamp down on a table.

'Ribadier!' I'll cry, 'Don't strike! Hear me out! A single word will exonerate me! Love! I love your wife; I must have her!'

THOMMEREUX falls to his knees before the sleeping angel.

Oh, Angèle!… My Angèle!… It's me! No, no… Don't push me away!…

(*to himself*) God, I'm stupid! She's asleep! Can't hear a word… (*calling*) Angèle!

He shakes her gently, then rather more forcibly.

ANGÈLE! Good Lord! Talk about Sleeping Beauty… I can't make love to her while she's unconscious! Well… No. Of course I can't!… ANGÈLE!!!… Nothing!…

(*getting up slowly*) What can I do? Think! My pistol! A few gunshots should do it… No, I don't think it will… Plus I'd stir up the whole house and damage the ceiling! Think!… Of course, how silly I am… Ribadier left me with instructions. 'Blow on her hands and she wakes up none the wiser.' Blowing does the job. Here goes…

He takes ANGÈLE's hands and blows on them.

Angèle!

ANGÈLE: Where am I? Oh, Good Lord, I fell asleep again. Why do I keep doing that?

THOMMEREUX falls painfully to his knees again.

THOMMEREUX: Ow!… Angèle!

THOMMEREUX puts his head in her lap and rubs his sore knees.

My Angèle!

ANGÈLE: (*pushing him off*) You! You, here!

THOMMEREUX: Yes, yes. It's me. No, no. Don't push me away. I'm tortured by guilt… Oh, to hell with petty bourgeois convention! Angèle, I love you!

ANGÈLE: (*getting up*) You're mad! What are you doing? Where's my husband?

ANGÈLE moves away. THOMMEREUX shuffles after her on his knees.

THOMMEREUX: Don't worry. He's gone out.

ANGÈLE: Where?

THOMMEREUX: To buy some cigars. He'd run out.

ANGÈLE: Oh, for Heaven's sake, get up! He'll be back any moment. The tobacconist's just next door.

THOMMEREUX: No, we've lots of time. He went to the Cuban place. They're stale, the ones they sell next door… Ah, Angèle!… I beg you! Listen to me!

ANGÈLE: You're insane. I won't hear a word.

THOMMEREUX: You must! Sweep conscience aside! Listen to your heart! I love you. You love me!

ANGÈLE: No. I don't love you.

THOMMEREUX: Yes, yes! You do!

THOMMEREUX struggles to his feet. ANGÈLE offers him a helping hand which he retains, kisses and holds to his cheek.

Think of that sultry afternoon. If it hadn't been for my timidity…you said so…

ANGÈLE: Well, I'm a warm-blooded woman!… I wasn't *in love* with you!

THOMMEREUX takes her in his arms.

THOMMEREUX: Weren't you?… Oh!… Angèle, I love you.

ANGÈLE disengages herself and moves off.

ANGÈLE: Let me go, Thommereux, I don't like it… And, you! His friend? A guest in his house? It's outrageous behaviour!

THOMMEREUX: Shocking, yes! But engagingly human! I'm flesh and blood, Angèle… My Angèle…

THOMMEREUX tries to take her in his arms again.

ANGÈLE: Get off!!… What's got into you! Think! Try telling yourself it would be the most hideous betrayal…

THOMMEREUX: Oh, I have… I've said it often… Ten…twenty times maybe…

ANGÈLE: And?

THOMMEREUX: By the twentieth time… I'd sort of got used to the idea.

ANGÈLE: Oh, you're unspeakable!… You'd given me your word of honour. You'd sworn you'd go back to Saigon!

THOMMEREUX: Ah! Ah! Go back to Saigon, she says. Slink off, tail between your legs… What? When my heart's brim-full of love and my body's throbbing with passion!?! You can't expect it of me!… Anyway, I'm not going…so, there!… Oh, you must have thought me a poor feeble wretch when I said I'd go!

ANGÈLE: Not at all. 'What a thoroughly decent and good-hearted chap!' were my exact words.

THOMMEREUX: 'What a perfect blundering fool!' were mine. Yes, yes, I know I did it once before…then I gave you up for Robineau, whom I loved like a brother. I won't do the same for all his successors…

ANGÈLE: Oh!

THOMMEREUX: And what good did going away do me? A certain swine took advantage of my absence to dispossess me! On returning, I found you annexed and myself cast aside… You were remarried…to a man who matched your linen!

ANGÈLE: Come along! Calm down!

THOMMEREUX: You knew I loved you. You belong to me. You're mine. He pinched you!

ANGÈLE: Thommereux!

THOMMEREUX stamps his foot like a spoilt child.

THOMMEREUX: Well, I want back what's mine! I want it now! I don't know if the law's on my side! I don't care. The law may condemn me!… I do know that I've been abused, that I've been robbed and that I intend to get back what's rightfully mine!

THOMMEREUX clasps her to him.

ANGÈLE: (*disengaging herself*) Thommereux, I beg you!

THOMMEREUX: I love you! I adore you, d'you hear! My heart's swollen with feeling; my head's swirling with poetry… I feel a verse coming on…

ANGÈLE: You!

THOMMEREUX: Yes! (*declaiming*)
'His love was passion's essence: as a tree
On fire by lightning with ethereal flame.
Kindled he was, and blasted...'

ANGÈLE: That's Byron!

THOMMEREUX: Is it? Yes, possibly. I never claimed
exclusive rights...

ANGÈLE: I see!

THOMMEREUX: Byron wrote it! I have lived it! Ah,
Angèle, tell me you love me!

ANGÈLE: All right, but on one condition.

THOMMEREUX: (*passionately*) What? May I hope... My
very life is yours... I'd kill myself if you asked me.
Right here, right now if I knew it would make you mine!

ANGÈLE: No, that's not necessary... Go back to Saigon,
that's all I ask.

THOMMEREUX: 'That's all,' she says! A mere nothing.
An epic journey across oceans and continents... Every
step taking me further away from you...

ANGÈLE: I'd know the true measure of your love.

THOMMEREUX: What? In kilometres!

ANGÈLE: Thommereux! You don't really love me!

THOMMEREUX: Yes, I do. That's why I don't want to
go... Oh, you don't know what you're asking... To cast
myself adrift...to grub a mean living among savages...
In the expectation of what exactly?... That, one fine day,
my turn will come... I'd be like some vulture, hovering,
circling, waiting for a man to die... An honest man... A
man who is, after all's said and done, a fellow human
being, if not my brother... No! No, my conscience
revolts at the whole idea... Hang around wishing

47

Ribadier were dead? Good God, let the man live! I'll take you right now and win his reprieve!

ANGÈLE: Oh, Thommereux, really!

THOMMEREUX: Plus one never really knows how long a husband will last…

ANGÈLE: Oh, oh… My poor Ribadier!

THOMMEREUX takes her around the waist.

THOMMEREUX: There! You see, you're moved… We should set up a nice little *ménage à trois*… All very calm. Very domestic. Everything arranged at his convenience, of course… We'd take great care of him…We'd humour him… He'd be the happiest of men! We two would deceive him but we'd all three love each other… Wouldn't that be Paradise?

ANGÈLE: (*moving away*) Are you mad?

THOMMEREUX: Me? No!… Why these scruples?… The most exemplary women have done it.

ANGÈLE: Oh!

THOMMEREUX: Absolutely. It's not been common knowledge, that's all… History's crawling with heroines who knew how to reconcile duty and desire… And then there's the Bible… You do have religious convictions, don't you?… Well, the Bible is full of examples –

ANGÈLE: – For instance?

THOMMEREUX: What?

ANGÈLE: *Ménages à trois* in the Bible. Name me one…

THOMMEREUX: Well… What about Ares and Aphrodite? It was years before Hephaestus found out!

ANGÈLE: They're Greeks!

THOMMEREUX: (*warming to the task*) All right. Well, then, there's…um… That's the plan, eh? Keep him talking… We're losing precious time… I love you, I tell you. I love you. (*seizing her*) Oh, passion's burning me up!

ANGÈLE: (*beating him off*) Stop it! Thommereux! Let me go!

THOMMEREUX: No, I won't. This hunger must be assuaged!

ANGÈLE: Ah! Stop or I'll scream!

ANGÈLE runs to the door leading to the hall.

Locked?

She runs to another door.

This one's locked too. And no key!

THOMMEREUX: No!

ANGÈLE: What's the meaning of this? Locked in my own house! It's outrageous! Thommereux, I demand that you open this door.

THOMMEREUX: No!

ANGÈLE: No? You've gone too far. Open it now!

THOMMEREUX: I don't have the key.

ANGÈLE: Huh?

THOMMEREUX: Your husband has it. He's the one who's locked you in!

ANGÈLE: My husband! Why?

THOMMEREUX: Now you're asking…

ANGÈLE: Right! Well, I still have the window.

THOMMEREUX positions himself between ANGÈLE and the window.

THOMMEREUX: Angèle, you can't.

ANGÈLE: Watch me!

THOMMEREUX: (*restraining her*) No!

ANGÈLE: Oh, God! Where is Ribadier? How long does it take to choose a cigar?

THOMMEREUX: Angèle! My Angèle! –

The doorbell rings – loud and insistent. THOMMEREUX and ANGÈLE freeze for a long moment.

What's that?

ANGÈLE: The door bell.

The doorbell is rung again, repeatedly.

That's my husband!

THOMMEREUX: (*aside*) It's her husband! Her husband's back. God, he's been quick. We're done for…

ANGÈLE: What's wrong with you?

THOMMEREUX: (*collapsing on the pouf*) Nothing. Nothing. Oh, my God, my God!…

Longer bursts of ringing from the doorbell.

ANGÈLE: Where's Sophie? Why doesn't she let him in?

THOMMEREUX gets up and starts pacing the room.

THOMMEREUX: Right! We're all right! It's all fine! We're all right! (*aside*) What's he going to say when he finds her awake?… He left her dead to the world… He'll twig immediately!… Oh, how ghastly!… I'll just have to hypnotize her myself… (*aloud*) Angèle, Angèle, come over here!

More ringing and hammering from outside – quite frantic now.

ANGÈLE: *(coming to him)* Why? What is it?… Sophie must have gone to bed.

THOMMEREUX: She keeps early hours!

ANGÈLE: Well, I'm locked in! I can't go…

THOMMEREUX: No! *(taking her hands)* Look into my eyes!

ANGÈLE: *(giggling)* Ha, ha! Oh, don't make me laugh…

THOMMEREUX: I'm not being funny. Stop laughing and start looking.

ANGÈLE: Oh. All right…

A beat.

THOMMEREUX: Are you sensing anything?

ANGÈLE: Oh, yes… There is something…

THOMMEREUX: *(aside)* She's sensing something… She is…

ANGÈLE: *(sniffing)* Yes… A sort of cosmetic smell…

THOMMEREUX: Ah! No. That'll be my hair… Oh, dear, oh dear, oh dear… I'm communicating with you telepathically… Can't you sense it? Don't you feel anything?

ANGÈLE: *(laughing again)* What is it you want me to feel?

THOMMEREUX: *(aside)* She feels nothing! *(aloud)* Try again. Come on, do it properly.

ANGÈLE: What?

THOMMEREUX: Eh? *Feel…* Try to *feel…* *(despairing)* Oh, forget it! Just forget it! *(resumes pacing)* I can't do it. I don't have the knack!

51

ANGÈLE: What are you trying to achieve?

*Voices, including RIBADIER's and SOPHIE's, from the hall.
RIBADIER is in the house.*

THOMMEREUX: In heaven's name, Angèle, just do
precisely what I tell you… Sit down there on the sofa…
When your husband comes in, pretend to be fast asleep.
Don't move a muscle till he wakes you himself.

ANGÈLE: (*draped on sofa*) I've no idea what this is all
about…

*THOMMEREUX takes the lamp and puts it back in its
original position.*

THOMMEREUX: I'll tell you later. Remember: whatever
you hear, don't react. Not a twitch, not a squeak…
Nothing, I beg you… The repercussions would be very,
very grave.

He dims the lamp.

ANGÈLE: What are you doing now?

THOMMEREUX: Putting everything back as it was… And
making a run for it. Not a sound, you understand.
Nothing. Just sleep…

*THOMMEREUX rushes out on to the balcony. He pauses a
moment, dithering over how far open to leave the window.*

*The commotion outside intensifies. THOMMEREUX, in a
panic, throws himself clumsily over the balustrade.*

A yelp of pain off-stage as he lands below.

Scene 2

ANGÈLE: (*alone*) Just sleep. Sleep! He's quite mad! But something's going on… Something very strange indeed.

The sound of a key in the lock and two distinct male voices outside.

It's my husband! And he's not alone! Oh, well, I'll sleep… Who knows? It might help solve the mystery.

RIBADIER, carrying a hat, bursts in and smartly shuts the door behind him barring the entrance. On the other side, SAVINET is trying to push his way in. A struggle ensues.

(*aside*) It's him.

ANGÈLE pretends to sleep.

RIBADIER: Really, Monsieur, have you finished?

SAVINET: (*from outside*) I'm coming in, I tell you.

RIBADIER: No!

SAVINET: Yes!

SAVINET hurls himself against the door and bursts in. SOPHIE, red-faced and in some disarray, follows.

RIBADIER: God in Heaven! What is it you want?

SAVINET is carrying another hat.

SAVINET: Got you, at last!

RIBADIER: Clearly… One moment. (*to SOPHIE*) Thank you, Sophie. Go back to bed.

SOPHIE smothers a giggle and exits. RIBADIER turns up the lamp and unlocks the two other doors, leaving the keys in locks.

ANGÈLE: (*aside*) What's going on?

RIBADIER: (*aside*) Angèle's still asleep, thank God! (*to SAVINET*) Right, Monsieur, kindly tell me the nature of your business here. I don't know you from Adam.

SAVINET: All right, Monsieur. No need to shout. I'll tell you why I'm here. But, first, ask your daughter to leave us.

RIBADIER: My daughter? Where? There! That's my wife!

SAVINET: Really! Then, ask your wife to go. What I have to say is for your ears alone.

RIBADIER: Oh, don't worry about her, Monsieur! My wife's sleeps like a log; you could fire a cannon in here and she wouldn't hear it.

SAVINET: Indeed? Well, Monsieur, not having a cannon to hand, I must take your word for it… I'm not going to beat about the bush. A word will suffice: I am Monsieur Savinet!

RIBADIER: Oh!!!

ANGÈLE: (*aside*) Savinet?

RIBADIER glances over to check ANGÈLE who hasn't stirred.

RIBADIER: So sorry, Monsieur. I'm still in the dark.

ANGÈLE: (*aside*) Me, too.

SAVINET: Really! Then I'll have to be more explicit, Monsieur. You are my wife's lover!

ANGÈLE jumps up and makes to leap on RIBADIER before thinking better of it and subsiding back on to the sofa.

RIBADIER: Me, Monsieur?

SAVINET: Yes, you!

ANGÈLE: (*aside*) Oh, the wretch!

ANGÈLE resumes her position, a slight smile on her lips, and watches RIBADIER.

SAVINET: You were with Madame Savinet just now when I returned rather inopportunely. You heard me arrive, got dressed in a hurry and made a quick dash for it out the back. Not quick enough, however… I was in hot pursuit; now I've tracked you down.

ANGÈLE: (*aside*) Beast! Bastard! Beastly bastard!

She subsides again. RIBADIER glances over at ANGÈLE before replying.

RIBADIER: I have no idea what you're talking about, Monsieur! There's been some terrible mistake. Your wife may well have a lover but it's not me!

SAVINET: Really!?! So, how come, Monsieur, you have my hat and I have yours?

SAVINET puts on the hat in his hand. It's far too small. Mechanically, RIBADIER follows suit. His hat is far too large.

You grabbed the wrong hat!

They exchange hats.

RIBADIER: Very well, Monsieur. Enough lies and evasions. It was me with Madame Savinet.

SAVINET: You admit it!

ANGÈLE jumps up as before, thinks better of it and falls back on to the sofa.

ANGÈLE: (*aside*) I'll kill him!

RIBADIER glances round again but ANGÈLE appears serene.

RIBADIER: So, Monsieur, what is it you're after?

SAVINET: What am I after? He asks what I'm after? Monsieur, you have made a complete fool of me!

RIBADIER: Now, come on!

SAVINET: Oh, yes, you have! I know: the cuckold is always a figure of fun. Absurd. Ridiculous. A laughing-stock… Well, Monsieur, I'm not normally a violent man – I'm a wine merchant – but if you ever breathe a word of this affair to anybody, I swear I will kill you!

RIBADIER: Huh?

SAVINET: Absolutely. I'm a peaceable sort, as a rule. I don't hold with armed combat: duels, that sort of thing… I mean, why do people do it? To satisfy society, that's why. Well, society knows nothing of this at the moment –

RIBADIER: – Certainly not!

SAVINET: Good! All I ask is that we keep it that way. In time I will divorce my wife and no-one will suspect the truth. I'm a respected wine merchant, Monsieur, and I won't allow scandal to prejudice my business affairs or cast a slur on my professional reputation.

RIBADIER: Surely, that wouldn't –

SAVINET: Oh, yes, it would! D'you know any Grand Masters of Wine? No. Well, believe me… If there were the least hint that I, that I were… It shows a lack of judgement, you see. If a man can't choose a good wife, how will he know a good vintage? No. I'd be finished in a week.

RIBADIER: Oh, rubbish –

SAVINET: – I must insist on your silence.

RIBADIER: Mere good manners require my discretion, Monsieur… Good Lord, man, you had to force it out of me!

SAVINET: True enough. (*wagging a finger*) One word and you're dead.

RIBADIER: Understood!... But, well, you keep assuming that you'd kill me. Don't you ever consider it might be the other way round?

SAVINET goes over to the drinks tray.

SAVINET: No, Monsieur. You don't have that right.

ANGÈLE: (*aside*) Lord! Will he never go?

SAVINET pours two small glasses of cognac from a decanter.

SAVINET: We injured husbands do have some prerogatives... That's only fair, after all... It's the lover's duty to allow himself to be killed... That's why – without being a fine swordsman or a great shot – I may say, with some confidence, that I shall kill you!

RIBADIER: Oh, but, excuse me... That's not a duel! That's an appointment with death!

SAVINET offers RIBADIER one of the glasses.

SAVINET: Sorry, old chap. Those are the rules.

RIBADIER: (*taking the glass*) Thank you!

They drink. RIBADIER sits on the arm of the sofa.

SAVINET: (*a change of tone*) It's rather good, this cognac. French?

RIBADIER: A Courvoisier!

SAVINET: D'you think so? It's good... Not pure. Blended... A little Armagnac, I think.

RIBADIER: Ah!

SAVINET: What did you pay for it?

RIBADIER: Eight francs.

SAVINET: (*putting down his glass*) Eight francs! (*to ANGÈLE*) You're being robbed! (*aside*) Oh, she's still asleep... (*aloud*) For six francs, I could find you one every bit as good and better.

RIBADIER: Really?

SAVINET: Absolutely! Would you like to try some? Send it back if you don't like it. I've got a few cases left...but you'll have to hurry.

RIBADIER: (*getting up*) Well, I wouldn't say no. (*aside*) Very decent of him...

ANGÈLE: (*aside*) What? Now they're doing a deal over cognac!

SAVINET pulls a notebook out of his pocket.

SAVINET: Let me know what you think... (*writing*) Right! For Monsieur...?

RIBADIER: Ribadier.

SAVINET: (*writing*) Ribadier...

RIBADIER: Shall I spell it?

SAVINET: Don't bother, Monsieur. I expect my wife knows your name... At least, I suppose she does... 'Ribadier: one case of '65' (*to RIBADIER*) Cash on delivery for a five per cent discount or twenty-eight days at the full price. It's up to you.

RIBADIER: Whatever's most convenient...

SAVINET: How very gracious!

ANGÈLE: (*aside*) On and on and on... Will he never go!

SAVINET: (*closing his book*) There! Done! We're all agreed, Monsieur.

RIBADIER: Absolutely!

SAVINET: A single word and you're dead.

RIBADIER: Eh? What? Oh, sorry!… Yes. Understood.

SAVINET: I'm always at your disposal. (*shaking hands*) Monsieur!

RIBADIER: Please. Allow me to show you out.

RIBADIER goes to the door. SAVINET picks up his hat.

SAVINET: Too kind!…

SAVINET looks curiously at ANGÈLE and shakes his head. Tentatively he prods her chest. ANGÈLE, eyes closed still, smartly slaps his hand away. SAVINET leaps back, bemused. He hastens to the door, stopping for a moment in front of the portrait.

What a fine painting! Van Dyke, no doubt… Is it one of your forbears?

RIBADIER moves back downstage.

RIBADIER: No, it's my wife's husband.

SAVINET: There's two of you!?!

RIBADIER: What? No. No, of course not. It's her first husband.

SAVINET: Ah! He cuts a fine figure… So you came along after… Oh, well… I wouldn't much care for that myself…

RIBADIER: And why not?

SAVINET: Well, for Number Two… It's a bit like being a servant picking at the left-overs from the master's table.

RIBADIER: (*dryly*) Indeed! I'd rather my position than yours any day, Monsieur.

SAVINET: Each to his own.

RIBADIER: (*aside*) Vulgar little man!

SAVINET: I must go.

> *RIBADIER escorts SAVINET towards the door. En route, SAVINET can't resist giving ANGÈLE another little prod. Aware of RIBADIER's eyes on her, she does not react this time.*

She's a champion sleeper, your wife! Quite dead to the world!

RIBADIER: This way, Monsieur.

SAVINET: Of course!

> *ANGÈLE snarls at his back.*

You must let me know if you ever need a good claret. Something special…

> *RIBADIER and SAVINET exit.*

Scene 3

ANGÈLE, furious, paces around the stage.

ANGÈLE: (*alone*) Oh! Oh! Oh! Oh!! The wretch! The swine! I don't know how I contained myself… I could have strangled him ten times over. Oh! Oh!! The swine! The swine! (*takes a deep breath*) Ah! It's so good to let it all out… (*picking up the thread*) So, that's where he gets his cigars! From the wife of that, that freak…who calmly flogs him cheap cognac… I bet it's vile… He's clearly taking advantage of the situation to off-load his worst stock… Fine! I'll force every last filthy drop down that bastard's throat! Ah! I'm fired up like a furnace and you, my dear, are going to feel the heat…

ANGÈLE stands by the fireplace as she sees RIBADIER re-enter the room. He seems very pleased with himself.

(*aside*) Him!

RIBADIER: Yes, goodbye, Monsieur. Goodbye! (*aside*) What a charming fellow: one word and… (*mimes cutting his throat*) Dead!…

RIBADIER humming happily, he makes for the sofa.

Time for wakey-wakeys…

ANGÈLE: I'll give you 'wakey-wakeys'!

RIBADIER jumps out of his skin.

RIBADIER: My wife!

ANGÈLE: Yes. Your wife!

RIBADIER: Awake! (*aside*) She's awake!

ANGÈLE: Ah! You weren't expecting to find me up and about, it seems?

RIBADIER: No! Yes! Why not?… (*aside*) How did she do that?

ANGÈLE: You traitor! You fiend! Where have you been? Go on. Tell me, or don't you dare?

RIBADIER: Where have I been?… Well, let me think –

ANGÈLE: – Liar!

RIBADIER: I haven't said anything yet! You want to know where I've been? Right. Good. Well, that's an interesting question you've raised. Let me address it in this way –

ANGÈLE: – Can't you ever give a straight answer?

RIBADIER: Well, that depends –

ANGÈLE: (*furiously*) – I'll tell you where you've been! With your mistress, Madame Savinet!

RIBADIER: Madame Savinet?

ANGÈLE: Don't pretend you don't know her! Her husband just left...

RIBADIER: Who? Oh, you mean, the gentleman who was here...

ANGÈLE: Yes, that fool!

RIBADIER: Oh, you know, that's really very funny... Ha, ha, ha!... You think I'm his wife's lover...

ANGÈLE: Certainly!

RIBADIER: (*laughing*) Ha, ha, ha!... How amusing that is!

ANGÈLE: Oh, do stop! It makes you look quite moronic.

RIBADIER: So you didn't get it?... Not straight away?

ANGÈLE: What?

RIBADIER: Oh, my poor darling, you didn't get it!

ANGÈLE: What? Tell me. Enough of this play-acting!

RIBADIER: (*aside*) Play-acting! (*aloud*) That's it! Precisely! Well done! We were rehearsing a play for the Club...and the man you saw just now...

ANGÈLE: Savinet, yes.

RIBADIER: Well, no, actually... That's not his name. He's called Baliveau!

ANGÈLE: Ah!

RIBADIER: Yes. Good old Baliveau! He's a member and – in this drama – he plays the role of Savinet, the deceived husband while I play the lover... I tried to get out of it but the President insisted: 'Only you can do it, Ribadier! No-one else has the looks or the physique!'

ANGÈLE: Really! You're the Club's resident Adonis, are you?

RIBADIER: Well, yes, I suppose I am…

ANGÈLE: That doesn't say much for the others!

RIBADIER: It was just a play, my love! A silly play!

ANGÈLE: Ah! I see! And wasn't it – some parts, at least – in verse?

RIBADIER: The whole thing, my darling! All in the most splendid verse!

ANGÈLE: You've got a huge hit on your hands… Some of those scenes…so true to life!

RIBADIER: I think so. (*aside*) I never thought I'd get off so lightly.

ANGÈLE: That scene, for example, where the lover gives the husband an order for cognac…

RIBADIER: Yes, isn't it priceless? That's the best bit, I think…

ANGÈLE: How does it go again?

RIBADIER: What? Oh! Oh?…

ANGÈLE: Recite some verses for me!

RIBADIER: Verses, darling? Really?… You want…in verse?

ANGÈLE: Yes. Chapter and verse.

RIBADIER: (*aside*) Christ! Lord knows, I can waffle… But not in verse! Not like this, off the top of my head!

ANGÈLE: Come on! Get on with it.

RIBADIER: Right… (*aside*) Damnfool idea to tell her it was in verse!

The doorbell rings.

Ah!

ANGÈLE, refusing to let him off so lightly, stations herself between RIBADIER and the door.

So… Where were we? Savinet steps forward and says to thingummy –

ANGÈLE: – The lover!

RIBADIER: Very good! Well remembered! (*aside*) Improvise, Ribadier! Panic be thy Muse!

ANGÈLE: So… What are you waiting for?

RIBADIER: All right, darling! Just finding the line… Er… Right. Yes, I've got it… So Savinet pours himself a drink and takes a sip:

'This brandy has a certain elegance…
Although, of course, it doesn't come from France.'

ANGÈLE: Yes, yes. I do remember him saying something like that.

RIBADIER: He did, didn't he? (*aside*) Oh, my God! Still, 'France' and 'Elegance'… Not bad.

ANGÈLE: Keep going…

RIBADIER: Of course. Ah…

Savinet says: 'And how much did you pay if I may ask?'

Me: 'Oh, only eight francs. Drawn straight from the cask.'

Him: 'That's steep, my friend. Take my advice,
I'll gladly sell you half a dozen, half the price.'

ANGÈLE: (*clapping her hands*) Wonderful! With a little change of metre at the end there?…

RIBADIER: Yes. It builds tension…

ANGÈLE: Go on…

RIBADIER: *(aside)* I'm surprising myself! I can do it!

ANGÈLE: Then, what happens?

RIBADIER: Well, I jump at it. Like a shot –

ANGÈLE: – In verse!

RIBADIER: Of course! That was just to give you the general idea…

The doorbell rings again, more insistently.

Ah!

RIBADIER is grateful for the diversion but ANGÈLE clearly has no intention of letting him off the hook.

Now, in the original text, how does it go?… Yes, I've got it:

'If brandy be the food of love, pour on.
I…er…wouldn't mind another little one.'

ANGÈLE: Magnificent. Who wrote this lyric masterpiece?

RIBADIER: Shakespeare, darling! Shakespeare! Didn't you recognize the style?

ANGÈLE: Not at all!

RIBADIER: Really! I thought it was quite obvious…

ANGÈLE: Remind me: which is the Shakespeare play with the wine merchant?

RIBADIER: Ah!… *The Vintner's Tale!*

ANGÈLE: Of course!… Anyway, it's a play. A play you were rehearsing… Good… That's all I wanted to know.

ANGÈLE heads for the door to her bedroom.

RIBADIER: Where are you going?

ANGÈLE: Nowhere special!

ANGÈLE exits.

Scene 4

RIBADIER: (*alone*) Ouf! What a business! Awake! She'd woken up! But how?… She couldn't have done it alone… Someone else must have… But who? Damned liberty whoever it was… (*light dawns*) Oh, the little worm!… What a snake!

THOMMEREUX his head round the door.

THOMMEREUX: May I come in?

RIBADIER: Of course! My friend! Come in. Come in!

THOMMEREUX enters, limping slightly and leaning on SOPHIE's arm. She is looking cross and even more dishevelled.

THOMMEREUX: (*aside*) His 'friend'? He knows nothing!

RIBADIER: Thank you, Sophie. Go back to bed.

SOPHIE stomps out.

You won't believe what's been happening! Some blighter woke up my wife while I was out!

THOMMEREUX: No?

RIBADIER: Yes!

THOMMEREUX: I find that hard to credit!

RIBADIER: Who? Who can it have been? I'm at a loss… (*seeing the open window*) Good God! The window's open. That's how he got in!

THOMMEREUX: Who?

RIBADIER: Him! The bastard who woke up my wife!

RIBADIER seizes THOMMEREUX by the throat.

This is what I'd like to do to him, that damned dog!

THOMMEREUX: Hey! Hey! You're hurting me!

RIBADIER: (*releasing him*) When I find him, I promise you, I'll beat him to a pulp!

THOMMEREUX: Ah! (*aside*) Now might be a good time to head back East.

The doorbell rings. Relieved, he makes for the door.

I'll get that, shall I?

RIBADIER: No. Sophie will go… (*eyeballing THOMMEREUX*) Thanks to him, my wife heard everything!… It put me right on the spot! There I was, composing poetry off the cuff…

THOMMEREUX: (*not understanding*) Ah!

RIBADIER: Politicians don't do poetry! It's not our thing… Oh! Some lines had too many beats; others didn't have enough…

THOMMEREUX: I expect they all balanced out in the end.

RIBADIER: Who cares? I don't think Angèle noticed…

RIBADIER slumps exhausted on to a sofa.

THOMMEREUX: (*aside*) No idea what he's on about…

RIBADIER: The whole thing was a nightmare! Quite ghastlya

SAVINET: (*off-stage*) Oh, Monsieur! Monsieur!

RIBADIER leaps up like a scalded cat.

RIBADIER: Aargh!

Scene 5

RIBADIER: What? Him! Here?

RIBADIER locks the door to ANGÈLE's bedroom. SAVINET enters from the hall, followed by a seething SOPHIE.

SAVINET: Monsieur! You're here. Thank God!

RIBADIER: What do you want? Thank you, Sophie. Go back to bed.

SOPHIE: WHAT'S THE POINT?

SOPHIE slams out. RIBADIER, THOMMEREUX and SAVINET exchange bemused glances over her strange outburst.

SAVINET: I need a word! First, ask your son to leave us.

RIBADIER: Him! He's not my son!

SAVINET: Not another husband, is he?

RIBADIER: Now you're just being silly! (*aside*) He will keep foisting children on me! Why?

SAVINET: Well, whatever, ask him to go!

RIBADIER shows THOMMEREUX the way to the dining room.

RIBADIER: (*to THOMMEREUX*) Would you mind awfully waiting through here for a moment…

THOMMEREUX: (*going*) Not at all… (*aside*) Who's he? Looks like trade. Some creditor perhaps…

THOMMEREUX exits.

RIBADIER: Right! Now, spit it out. What d'you want?

SAVINET: Come with me!

RIBADIER: Where?

SAVINET: To my wife!

RIBADIER: Er, no, thanks all the same. Not tonight.

SAVINET: Yes, tonight. Now. It's an emergency! Ouf! What is this strange effect you have on women?

RIBADIER: Why d'you ask?

SAVINET: Why? My wife's fast asleep, Monsieur, and
    I can't wake her up.

RIBADIER: (*with a certain pride*) She may well be tired –

SAVINET: – She's completely catatonic! Just like your
    wife…

RIBADIER: (*aside*) Oh, my God!

SAVINET: And in such a state of undress! You'll forgive
    me if I don't go into details…

RIBADIER: (*aside*) That must have been me! I was in such
    a staring panic… I must have caught her eye and sent
    her off! (*aloud*) What did you do then?

SAVINET: (*shrugging*) I looked at her and said: 'That's my
    wife!'

RIBADIER: No! I mean, didn't you try to rouse her?

SAVINET: Of course, I did! I've been half an hour shouting
    and shaking her… Nothing… Then, I said to myself: that
    man, Ribadier, is mixed up in this… I just said 'Ribadier'
    like that because you weren't there…

RIBADIER: Yes. Of course. It doesn't matter.

SAVINET: Come with me!

*SAVINET tries to drag RIBADIER along with him.
ANGÈLE, off-stage, tries to open her bedroom door.*

RIBADIER: That's Angèle! Oh, for pity's sake! Go now!
    You don't need me. You can wake her yourself.

SAVINET: How?

RIBADIER: Sssh! Keep it down!

SAVINET: (*stage whisper*) How?

RIBADIER: Blow on her hands.

SAVINET: Blow on her hands! I'll give it a try.

ANGÈLE, off-stage, struggles vigorously with the door. SAVINET makes to leave.

RIBADIER: Phew!

RIBADIER heads towards ANGÈLE's bedroom.

SAVINET: (*shouts from the door*) Right or left?

RIBADIER: Lower, please! What?

SAVINET: (*stage whisper*) Which hand should I blow on? Right or left?

RIBADIER: Either or both. Doesn't matter.

SAVINET turns away. The rattling and shaking at ANGÈLE's door increases. At the last moment, SAVINET turns back again.

SAVINET: (*loud*) Tell me, should I blow hot or cold?

RIBADIER: Sssh! God, has the man no volume control?

SAVINET: (*stage whisper*) Should I blow hot or cold?

RIBADIER: (*exasperated; shouting*) Hot or cold! Doesn't matter! Either works!

SAVINET: No need to shout…

SAVINET exits.

Scene 6

RIBADIER: Stand well back…

RIBADIER unlocks the door. ANGÈLE, wearing a hat and carrying her bag and umbrella, erupts furiously into the room.

ANGÈLE: What on earth are you playing at? Didn't you hear me?

RIBADIER: No. Nothing… You're going out?

ANGÈLE: (*heading for the door*) Yes!

RIBADIER: (*anxious*) Where are you going?

ANGÈLE: Where? To your Club, dear. I want to book two seats for your performance.. The best in the house!

RIBADIER: You can't!!… Men only. No women. Strict rule, I'm afraid.

ANGÈLE: (*turning back*) How long are you going to keep this up?

RIBADIER: Sorry?

ANGÈLE: This farce.

RIBADIER: I'm not with you.

ANGÈLE: D'you really suppose you had me fooled for an instant? I know what I heard! You have a mistress!

RIBADIER: Me?

ANGÈLE: Yes, you! And I'm off to let the world in on your secret: Eugène Ribadier, Senator of the Third Republic, and Madame Savinet, wife of a wine merchant, are lovers!

RIBADIER: Wretched woman! You can't!

ANGÈLE: I can and I will!

RIBADIER: (*aside*) She wants to kill me! She wants to see me slain! (*aloud*) Angèle, I beg you to consider the consequences.

ANGÈLE: What consequences? You'll be dead. I'll be free. Somehow the Republic will struggle on without you… So, what?

ANGÈLE makes for the door. RIBADIER bars her way.

RIBADIER: Angèle, you wouldn't…

ANGÈLE: Oh, but I would…

RIBADIER: You won't…

ANGÈLE: (*backing towards the sofa*) I will… I will… I will…

RIBADIER: Listen to me: you're not going out!

ANGÈLE: Yes, yes, I am….

Gradually, ANGÈLE is mesmerised by RIBADIER. Subdued, she falls back asleep on to the sofa.

RIBADIER: That's right! You stay there… Oh! Good Lord, I've put her under without meaning to… (*he is about to blow on her hands, then thinks better of it*) Hey!… Never mind… That's rather convenient, as it happens… I could leave her asleep for years…ten, maybe; fifteen, even… Quite peaceful with her hat and her umbrella… She might forget all about it… Of course, she's rather in the way just there… I know, I could put her away upstairs in a spare bedroom… (*shaking himself*) No. No, I can't, it's not practical… Oh, dear God! How am I going to wangle my way out of this one!?!

Scene 7

THOMMEREUX puts his head round the dining room door.

THOMMEREUX: Hallo! Forgotten me in here?

RIBADIER: (*aside*) Oh, what a brilliant idea! (*aloud*) Come in. Come here…

THOMMEREUX: (*advancing*) Me? (*seeing ANGÈLE*) Ah! Nodded off again, I see!

RIBADIER produces a folded card table and sets it up.

RIBADIER: Yes. Right. Sit yourself down here. We're going to play cards.

THOMMEREUX: What? At this hour? Why?

RIBADIER finds a pack of cards in the sideboard.

RIBADIER: It's part of my plan. (*forcing him to sit*) Not a moment to lose.

THOMMEREUX: But I don't know any card games.

RIBADIER: Doesn't matter. I shall win anyway.

THOMMEREUX: (*huffily*) I'm not playing if it's rigged from the start –

THOMMEREUX breaks off, seeing RIBADIER remove ANGÈLE's hat, bag and umbrella.

What are you doing?

RIBADIER: Undressing her.

THOMMEREUX: Here!?! Now!?!

RIBADIER: I am simply tidying away certain of my wife's belongings.

RIBADIER puts ANGÈLE's things away in the windowseat. He considers her sleeping figure.

Now... Have I thought of everything? Ah!

RIBADIER picks up the work basket from the sofa and puts it on ANGÈLE's knees. He places a piece of tapestry in her hand and tries to thread a needle. Failing, he shrugs and inserts the unthreaded needle between ANGÈLE's thumb and forefinger.

THOMMEREUX: I'll be damned if I know what's going on!

RIBADIER: Haven't you guessed? My wife knows everything!

THOMMEREUX: Oh, no!

RIBADIER: This is my only chance. Right. You shuffle...

RIBADIER sits down opposite THOMMEREUX.

THOMMEREUX: Oh, all right!

THOMMEREUX makes an inept attempt to shuffle, dropping some of the cards.

I don't see how a game of cards helps –

RIBADIER snatches the pack from him.

RIBADIER: Don't you understand? (*shuffling expertly*) We're playing for my wife!

THOMMEREUX: At cards! No. No, really!… Why not dominoes? I'm rather good at that!

RIBADIER: What are you talking about? We're playing for my wife… We're going to put her off the scent!

THOMMEREUX: Right! (*aside*) Not a clue what he's up to…

RIBADIER: Here we go. Just do as I say; say as I do…

THOMMEREUX: Got it. (*aside*) Where's this all going?

RIBADIER: I'll deal!

THOMMEREUX: I'll deal!

RIBADIER: No, I will!

THOMMEREUX: No, I will!

RIBADIER: (*passing him the cards*) As you wish…

THOMMEREUX: As you wish…

RIBADIER: Now, come on. We've got to decide.

THOMMEREUX: Now, come on. We've got to decide.

RIBADIER: Oh, really! That's enough! What's your game, repeating my every word!

THOMMEREUX: You told me to –

RIBADIER: – God, you're stupid! Not now. When my wife wakes up… Whatever I say or do, just follow suit…

THOMMEREUX: (*huffy*) I've told you I don't play cards.

RIBADIER: No! I meant, 'play along with'…back up, second, endorse, support, confirm, ratify –

THOMMEREUX: – Ah! I see. Forgive me! I'm an ordinary plain-speaking citizen. 'Do as I say, say as I do' in my book means… Well! Never mind! I'm with you now…

RIBADIER: (*dealing the cards*) Off we go!

THOMMEREUX scoops up his cards inexpertly and holds them in an untidy fan.

THOMMEREUX: Fine. But, remember, I don't know how to play –

RIBADIER: (*getting up*) – Yes. Yes.

RIBADIER blows twice on ANGÈLE's hands; she stirs and wakes slowly. RIBADIER quickly sits back down opposite THOMMEREUX.

(*aside*) Ready? (*aloud*) Ah, ha! Hearts are trumps! And I have the King!

THOMMEREUX: Just one? I've got two!

RIBADIER: Shut up! (*aside*) What an ass!

ANGÈLE: Where am I? What happened?

RIBADIER: Hearts!

THOMMEREUX: (*low, to RIBADIER*) Hey! When's it my turn?

ANGÈLE: Eugène! What's he doing? Playing cards with Thommereux!

RIBADIER: Hearts!... Another trump!

THOMMEREUX: What? That's not fair!

ANGÈLE: What on earth's going on?

RIBADIER: And another...! That makes five! I win!

THOMMEREUX throws his cards sulkily on the table.

THOMMEREUX: Oh! You're just making up the rules as
you go along!

ANGÈLE: (*calling*) Eugène!

RIBADIER: (*to THOMMEREUX*) Sssh! (*turning to
ANGÈLE*) Ah! Did you have a nice sleep, darling?

ANGÈLE: What? I've been sleeping...?

RIBADIER: Well, yes!... You've had about an hour's nap!

ANGÈLE: I've had...? Really? Not again!

*ANGÈLE shuts her eyes, then opens them wide as she tries to
pull herself together.*

THOMMEREUX: (*aside*) Ah! Light dawns... Oh,
Thommereux! This could all go horribly wrong.

*ANGÈLE gapes at the tapestry then starts searching for her
things.*

ANGÈLE: They've gone! Where? Where are they?... My
bag and hat!

RIBADIER: What?

ANGÈLE: What have I done with my hat and bag?

RIBADIER: What have you done with them? Did you have
them with you?

THOMMEREUX: (*aside*) Oh, he's good! Nerves of steel!
Quite shameless...

ANGÈLE: Didn't I have them?

RIBADIER: What! To take a nap! I didn't see them...

ANGÈLE: I don't understand...

ANGÈLE puts her hand to her forehead as she tries to remember.

THOMMEREUX: (*aside*) What a con-man! So glib! So convincing!

RIBADIER: I don't think you've quite woken up yet...

ANGÈLE: Maybe not... Have I gone mad?

RIBADIER: (*low, to THOMMEREUX*) It's working...

THOMMEREUX: (*low, to RIBADIER*) What a performance! You're a master!

RIBADIER: (*low, to THOMMEREUX*) Thank you. It's a gift I have.

ANGÈLE: So, you haven't just been out?

RIBADIER: Me! (*laughing*) D'you hear that, Thommereux? No. We've been here the whole evening, playing cards.

THOMMEREUX: And he's been cheating all night!

RIBADIER: Excuse me!

THOMMEREUX: (*low*) Lends a certain authenticity...

ANGÈLE: There wasn't a man here?

RIBADIER: A man?

ANGÈLE: Yes. A Monsieur Savinet.

RIBADIER: Savinet? (*to THOMMEREUX*) I don't think I know a Savinet. Do you?

THOMMEREUX: Savinet? No... Oh, wait a moment!

Wasn't there a Savinet during Louis XI's reign?… A cousin of Joan of Arc?…

ANGÈLE: No. This one's wife is Eugène's mistress.

THOMMEREUX: Oh, him! No, I don't know him.

RIBADIER: My mistress!!! (*laughing*) Oh, she is drôle! That's funny! Ha, ha, ha! Ho, ho, ho… (*to THOMMEREUX*) I have a *mistress!* D'you hear that?

THOMMEREUX: (*laughing too*) You! A mistress!… Tee hee, hee, hee, hee!

ANGÈLE: So…what? It's really not true?

RIBADIER: D'you have to ask? Lord, the things you come up with!

ANGÈLE: It's not true! (*bursts out laughing*) Ah, ha, ha, ha, ha!

RIBADIER and THOMMEREUX are, apparently, convulsed with laughter.

RIBADIER / THOMMEREUX: Ah, ho, ho, ho, ho! Tee, hee, hee, hee!

RIBADIER: (*low*) It's working!

THOMMEREUX: (*low*) Yes! But where's it going?

ANGÈLE: Then it must have been a dream! Oh, you've no idea…what a bizarre dream!

RIBADIER: (*laughing*) You had a dream?… (*to THOMMEREUX*) My wife's been dreaming!

THOMMEREUX: (*laughing*) Yes! She certainly has…

ANGÈLE: (*laughing*) You had a mistress…

Fresh explosions of laughter from RIBADIER and THOMMEREUX.

Wait! You don't know what happened yet!… Her
husband caught you red-handed… His name was
Savinet; I don't know why…

RIBADIER: (*laughing hysterically*) Savinet! What a funny name!

THOMMEREUX: Hilarious!

ANGÈLE: Anyway, he followed you here… Confronted
you, sold you some cognac and left… Then you made up
some dreadful doggerel…

THOMMEREUX: Oh, it's to die for! I'm getting quite
hysterical…

*THOMMEREUX sobers suddenly while RIBADIER
continues to guffaw noisily.*

Oh, la, la!

RIBADIER: (*laughing*) Go on! Go on!

ANGÈLE: So, you'd gone off out to your mistress… And
I was alone.

ANGÈLE laughs. THOMMEREUX looks panic-stricken.

RIBADIER: Yes. Yes…

THOMMEREUX: (*aside*) Oh, my God! Thin ice alert!

RIBADIER: And then?

ANGÈLE: Then… No, no, I can't tell you in front of
Monsieur Thommereux.

THOMMEREUX: No, don't! I wouldn't want you to.
Delicacy of feeling. I quite understand…

ANGÈLE: I don't mean to be rude… It was just a foolish
dream. Nothing you should know…

THOMMEREUX: Not a problem. Believe me, I'm quite
happy here in the dark.

ANGÈLE: I'll tell my husband when we're alone.

THOMMEREUX: (*aside*) Oh, la, la! Saigon, here I come.

ANGÈLE: Oh, I don't suppose it matters... I thought... (*laughing*) Oh, dreams can be so silly and embarrassing...

RIBADIER: (*still convulsed*) Oh, quite absurd, can't they, Thommereux?

THOMMEREUX: (*pretending to laugh*) Completely absurd! Entirely ludicrous! Utterly delusional! Tee, hee, hee!

ANGÈLE: (*laughing*) The wine merchant!...

RIBADIER: (*laughing*) Savinet!...

THOMMEREUX: A cousin of Joan of Arc!...

ALL: Ha, ha, ha! Ho, ho, ho! Tee, hee, hee...

All three are splitting their sides – each in their own manner according to their situation and personality.

SAVINET appears at the door. Infected by their unbridled hilarity, he begins to laugh too.

Scene 8

Finally ANGÈLE, RIBADIER and THOMMEREUX notice SAVINET and leap to their feet.

ALL: Savinet!

ANGÈLE: Ah, ah, ah! So he's not a figment of my imagination!

SAVINET: What's the matter with them all?

RIBADIER: (*appalled*) What do you want, you wretched man? What do you want?

SAVINET: I tried everything: hot, cold, right, left, together... Nothing worked! I had to come!

ANGÈLE goes to SAVINET.

ANGÈLE: So, Monsieur, it is for real. Your wife is my husband's mistress!

SAVINET: *WHAT? HE TOLD YOU!…*

SAVINET rounds threateningly on RIBADIER.

RIBADIER: Oh, go to hell! (*to ANGÈLE*) Angèle, I can explain…

ANGÈLE: Leave me alone, Monsieur! It's all over between us!

SAVINET marches up to RIBADIER who has collapsed on to the pouf.

SAVINET: You have betrayed me, Monsieur. You know the penalty! Death at my hand! I must kill you!

End of Act Two.

ACT THREE

Scene 1

Strong morning sunlight. Coffee cups etc. THOMMEREUX paces the room; RIBADIER is slumped on a sofa.

THOMMEREUX: (*happily*) Poor old chap! It's pistols for two and coffee for one... A fight to the death... Survival of the fittest!...

RIBADIER shoots him a dirty look.

RIBADIER: Bah!... Hardly! I am obliged to give him satisfaction apparently! My hands are tied... I just stand there: target practice... (*rallying*) Still, my friend, *nil desperandum!* There's always hope; one never quite knows how things may turn out...

THOMMEREUX: No. One never knows... He might turn the gun on himself!

RIBADIER shoots him another dirty look.

RIBADIER: In case things do go wrong, please take this letter. It contains my last wishes...

THOMMEREUX: Your last wishes?

RIBADIER: Yes! Not a cheerful document... It's painful to confront one's own mortality... (*handing him the letter*) There you are... I thought of you.

THOMMEREUX: What? Me? As your... Is it possible?

RIBADIER: Yes. I thought you could deliver it to my wife if, well, what we know may happen does indeed occur...

THOMMEREUX: Oh! Right! (*aside*) I knew it was too good to be true...

RIBADIER: May I count on you?

THOMMEREUX: Don't worry. She'll have it like a shot!

RIBADIER shoots THOMMEREUX a baleful glance.

RIBADIER: It's a dead cert, is it?… (*bitter laugh*) Or, rather, I'm a dead cert…

THOMMEREUX: Is that everything?

RIBADIER: No. There's another letter.

THOMMEREUX: Another? (*side*) Now I'm his postman!

RIBADIER: (*getting up*) It's for the President of my Club. Asking him to be my second. My second second…

THOMMEREUX: (*getting up*) I see.

RIBADIER: Yes. He's a bit gaga…but, well, he is President. Would you go and deliver it for me?

THOMMEREUX: But if he's really gaga…

RIBADIER: Well, you decide what's best when you meet him… I entrust you with all my affairs.

THOMMEREUX: Right-y-oh! I'll be off then.

RIBADIER: (*lugubriously*) As for the rest… Well, I must trust in the Lord!

THOMMEREUX: Hallelujah!

THOMMEREUX exits, whistling merrily.

Scene 2

RIBADIER: (*alone*) How can he whistle at a time like this? Mind you, I'd whistle if I were just a witness… Oh, God, this duel!

SOPHIE enters.

Ah! Sophie!

SOPHIE: Monsieur?

RIBADIER: Have two gentlemen, all in black, been asking for me?

SOPHIE: All in black?… Is Monsieur burying someone?

RIBADIER: No. No yet. They're witnesses.

SOPHIE: Is Monsieur marrying someone?

RIBADIER: No, Sophie. My poor Sophie! I am fighting a duel!

SOPHIE bursts out laughing.

SOPHIE: Monsieur's fighting a duel! Ha, ha, ha! God, that's hilarious!

RIBADIER: (*piqued*) Really? Why, may I ask?

SOPHIE: (*laughing*) I just can't see it! Ho, ho, ho…

RIBADIER: I'm not asking you to exercise your feeble imagination, Sophie, merely to inform me when these gentlemen arrive.

SOPHIE tries to stifle her giggles.

SOPHIE: Yes, Monsieur. Of course.

RIBADIER: (*aside*) Everyone's curiously jolly about my impending demise…

RIBADIER exits.

Scene 3

SOPHIE: (*aside*) He's fighting a duel! Men! They never grow up… Daft as brushes!

ANGÈLE enters from her bedroom.

ANGÈLE: Ah! Sophie! Is Monsieur not up yet?

SOPHIE: Oh, yes, Madame. Should I tell him you're dressed?

ANGÈLE: No. Please. Don't tell anyone.

SOPHIE: Very good, Madame.

SOPHIE exits.

ANGÈLE: (*alone*) He's the last person I want to see…

Scene 4

ANGÈLE: (*alone*) What a fool he's made of me!… How could he?… To abuse his wife's innocent slumber… Why do I keep nodding off though? It's very odd… Perhaps I should see a doctor… Anyway, it's outrageous behaviour!… I can't help feeling there's still something in all this I don't know…

Scene 5

SOPHIE: (*from the door*) Monsieur Savinet.

ANGÈLE: Eh?

SOPHIE: This way, Monsieur; Madame is at home.

SAVINET: (*entering*) Ah! Madame. Good morning!

SOPHIE exits.

ANGÈLE: You're here, Monsieur… After what's happened?

SAVINET advances downstage and deposits his hat.

SAVINET: I realize, Madame, that my presence is a little, er, unconventional. I know: one may only communicate with one's opponent in a duel through the respective witnesses… Rules! Who made 'em up, I'd like to know… Anyway, I was never consulted, so I'm disregarding them.

ANGÈLE: Ah!

SAVINET: Besides, I particularly wish to speak to
Monsieur Ribadier before our seconds meet. But I can
tell you just as easily… I caught Monsieur Ribadier, did
I not, with my wife… *In flagrante*…

ANGÈLE: Yes! The predatory brute!

SAVINET: Ah, Madame! If only my wife had said the
same. But she didn't… And what's done is done… The
milk has been spilt… I behaved towards Monsieur
Ribadier with perfect chivalry. I only made one
condition: that we keep it strictly between ourselves…

ANGÈLE: You could hardly have been more generous!

SAVINET: No, I don't think so. But he broke his word!

ANGÈLE: To be fair, Monsieur, he only told me and
I forced it out of him –

SAVINET: – True. But if a man will tell his own wife of
his adultery, who won't he tell? No, I'm sorry. Now third
parties have become involved, I consider a duel
inevitable. Now, Madame, to the point: those in the know
know anyway. But those not in the know needn't know.
And I'd rather they didn't… I'd hate to draw attention to
myself with the Grand Masters…

ANGÈLE: You're very modest.

SAVINET: A wine merchant thrives as one of the crowd:
solid, orthodox, reliable… So I came to ask good old
Ribadier if he'd keep the real reason for our meeting
secret from his seconds and everyone. We shall fight
under some other pretext… For example, Ribadier and
I quarrelled over dinner; a fine wine was served and
Ribadier insisted that it was a Bordeaux when I'd already
pronounced it a Burgundy. Result: mortal combat!

ANGÈLE: D'you find that convincing?

SAVINET: Absolutely! The Grand Masters would appreciate a matter of professional honour.

ANGÈLE: Whatever… You must discuss it with Monsieur Ribadier. I no longer have anything to do with him.

ANGÈLE sits on the sofa. SAVINET takes a seat next to her.

SAVINET: What's this? Ah! You're not still cross with him?

ANGÈLE: 'Cross' doesn't begin to describe how I feel.

SAVINET: Oh! You should try being a little more philosophical about it: nothing's either good or bad but thinking makes it so…

ANGÈLE: Don't you start…

SAVINET: Oh, I didn't feel like this at first! No! I was incandescent, just like you… But then, one calms down, one reflects… One remembers that the most important thing in life is to establish an agreeable situation for oneself and to hang on to it… This morning when my servant brought up my breakfast tray and handed over my letters, I said to myself: 'Has anything really changed?' No. Not really. It's all a question of perception… Moral codes! Who made 'em up, I'd like to know… A lot of silly cant and convention in my view.

ANGÈLE: D'you think so?

SAVINET: Absolutely… My wife's been much nicer to me since I found out. Yes! Domestic life's much more pleasant.

ANGÈLE: (*getting up*) It appears you're in my husband's debt, Monsieur!

SAVINET: Oh, I wouldn't go that far… Not only was he prepared to make off with my wife, but he spoke about me most disrespectfully too.

ANGÈLE: No!

SAVINET: Look!

SAVINET pulls a letter out of his pocket.

ANGÈLE: What's that?

SAVINET: It's a letter from your husband to my wife that I came across…

ANGÈLE: How?

SAVINET: A systematic search. Listen to this.

ANGÈLE: Oh!

SAVINET: (*reading*) 'My Réré!' It's an abbreviation of Thérèse! My wife's name is Thérèse.

ANGÈLE: Ah!

SAVINET: *I* call her 'Théthé'. I took the first syllable and he took the second…

ANGÈLE: I'll give him 'Réré'!

SAVINET: Too late for that, Madame!… (*reading*) 'My Réré, We've only just parted but I simply had to write: what a deliriously happy evening…'

ANGÈLE: Oh! It's quite indecent!

SAVINET: Indeed! Tell me about it. (*reading*) 'I know you can't love your husband, he is…' (*to ANGÈLE*) No. You read it. Here. Read it. I'd rather you did it than me.

ANGÈLE: (*reading*) 'I know you can't love your husband; he's as ugly as sin…'

SAVINET: That's me he's talking about… Not very polite, is it?

ANGÈLE: (*reading*) 'How lucky he is to have such an adorable wife...' Oh! 'When I compare you with mine who is...' (*to SAVINET*) No. Here. You read it. I can't!

SAVINET: (*reading*) '...Who is intolerable!'

ANGÈLE: Oh!

SAVINET: (*reading*) 'Suspicious!'

ANGÈLE: Oh!

SAVINET: (*reading*) 'And a terrible nag!'

ANGÈLE: (*furious*) Oh!

SAVINET: (*reading*) 'She could be quite a problem if it weren't for my clever little ruse.

ANGÈLE: Eh?

SAVINET: (*reading*) 'It's delightfully simple... Every time your...' Oh! Now it's my turn again... (*reading*) 'Every time your...' No. I can't... Here.

ANGÈLE: (*taking the letter*) 'Every time your idiotic husband goes away...'

SAVINET: That's me again. Not very polite, is it?

ANGÈLE: (*reading*) 'I simply look my wife straight in the eye and she falls asleep for as long as I need...'

SAVINET: He's done it to mine too.

ANGÈLE: Hey?.. What?... Me?... Oh, the monster! Now I see...all those inexplicable naps!... I was... He was... Oh, the unspeakable fiend!

SAVINET: Read! Read the next bit!

ANGÈLE: No. No, I can't go on.

ANGÈLE gives SAVINET the letter.

SAVINET: (*reading*) 'Nothing can disturb our love-making!'

ANGÈLE: Oh!

SAVINET: (*reading*) 'If you knew how I love you...'

ANGÈLE: (*furious*) How I love you! Did you ever...?

Instinctively, she slaps SAVINET round the face.

SAVINET: (*furious*) Madame!

ANGÈLE: Oh, I'm so sorry. I thought you were my husband.

SAVINET: He may have taken over my role at home, Madame, but that's no reason for me to substitute for him here!

ANGÈLE: Oh, this is all beside the point! Anyway, I'll have the letter. I can make use of it.

ANGÈLE snatches the letter from SAVINET.

SAVINET: Excuse me! So can I... I want it!

ANGÈLE: Forgive me, but the letter is written by my husband: it belongs to me.

SAVINET: Forgive me, but the letter was written to my wife: it belongs to me!

ANGÈLE: Oh, all right, then! We get half each.

ANGÈLE tears the letter in two and gives SAVINET one half.

SAVINET: (*aside*) My half's blank...

ANGÈLE: Oh, the sadistic wretch! He hypnotized me! I'd never have believed him capable... But, well, there it is, in black and white... He hypnotized me against my will!... Oh, now I know exactly what I must do.

SAVINET: Me, too!

ANGÈLE: Divorce!

SAVINET: Me, too!

ANGÈLE: I'll go and live all alone.

SAVINET: Me, too!

ANGÈLE: I'll make him give back my dowry...

SAVINET: Me, too! Eh?

ANGÈLE: I said: I'll make him give back my dowry.

SAVINET: Oh, I heard you. So you think that –

ANGÈLE: – I should bloody well hope so! He's not keeping it once we've separated!

SAVINET: That sounds fair... Damn, damn, damn!

ANGÈLE: What's the matter?

SAVINET: Nothing as far as your husband's concerned. I speak on my own account: damn, damn, damn!

ANGÈLE: What is it?

SAVINET: My wife came with four hundred thousand francs and I invested the lot in Argentine stocks...

ANGÈLE: So?

SAVINET: Well, at the time, they were doing fine. Today they're down seventy-five per cent... It's not the moment to sell. I wouldn't be able to give her a full refund.

ANGÈLE: You have your personal fortune.

SAVINET: It's all tied up in my business.

ANGÈLE: Wind it up. Liquidate your assets.

SAVINET: It's easy for you to talk... Hah! It's not enough for Monsieur Ribadier and my wife to cu..., to cu...cu... Hum... To do what they did to me...Ouf!... No. That cost me dear... But now it's going to cost me money! Ah, no, I can't bear it!

ANGÈLE: (*impatiently*) Oh, really!

SAVINET: No, no! I want things back as they were, or at least, to appear so…

ANGÈLE: It's no one's business but yours.

SAVINET: (*retrieving his hat*) Yes! I'm going to find Théthé…

ANGÈLE: Théthé?…

SAVINET: My wife.

ANGÈLE: Oh, yes! Réré for my husband.

SAVINET: Réré for him! Théthé for me. I'm going to find Théthé and clear the air with her. Would you apologize to dear Ribadier and say I couldn't wait any longer for him?

ANGÈLE: I'll tell him.

SAVINET: If you'd be so kind. Right, goodbye, Madame.

SAVINET makes for the door, then turns back.

You know, Madame, whatever we say, a duel will arouse comment. You're the only one who knows… If I may rely on your discretion, perhaps there's no need for us to fight…

ANGÈLE: Oh?… Really?…

ANGÈLE smiles, realizing this condition might prove useful to her.

(*enjoying the moment*) Let me think about it.

SAVINET: I'll wait to hear. Now I'm off to hear my wife's excuses… (*aside*) Not that there are any really… But Argentine stocks were worth three hundred and fifty-seven francs yesterday. I can't sell them at that price.

SAVINET exits.

ANGÈLE: (*alone*) Yes! Go on. Accept any old whitewash! (*getting up*) That's men for you! Not so women! Ribadier won't wriggle out of this one! No! Nothing he can say will mollify me!… Ah! Ah! You used to hypnotize me! How very convenient! Madame is in the way; put her to sleep and tidy her away. Right! *À nous deux!* Time to turn the tables. Time for a little poetic justice!

RIBADIER enters.

(*aside*) Him! Right on cue!

RIBADIER: (*aside*) My wife! (*aloud*) I beg your pardon, Madame. Sophie had told me there was a gentleman waiting…

ANGÈLE: Let's not bother about him. He couldn't wait and he went… I want to talk to you.

RIBADIER: To me?

ANGÈLE: About the most serious matter!

RIBADIER: Oh, Madame, I can guess what you want to say. I am entirely to blame. You'd be perfectly justified in divorcing me…

ANGÈLE: Er, no, actually… That wasn't it. We can't get divorced. Something has happened – so shocking and shameful – that I can't get divorced however I may feel.

RIBADIER: What are you saying?

ANGÈLE: It's true, isn't it, that you've been putting me to sleep all those evenings when you were…?

RIBADIER: What? You know?… I won't try to lie about it. Yes, it's true.

ANGÈLE: (*aside*) He admits it! (*aloud*) Well, Monsieur, each time – once I was asleep and you had gone – a man found his way in here.

RIBADIER: What do you mean?

ANGÈLE: Well, that, under cover of darkness and by taking unfair advantage of my…my –

RIBADIER: (*leaping up*) – It's not true! Tell me it's not true!

ANGÈLE: Alas! I wish it weren't…

RIBADIER: Oh, my God!… Yes, I see now! Yesterday: the open window! That's how he got in, the bastard! (*to ANGÈLE*) Who is he? What's his name?

ANGÈLE: I don't know!

RIBADIER: Didn't you recognise him? You saw him!

ANGÈLE: No, I didn't. The lamp was always low.

RIBADIER: Oh, it's appalling!… So, every single time I…this man… Who knows if it were just the one…? There may have been several!

ANGÈLE: Oh, no! I do know it was always the same one!

RIBADIER: Oh, stop, stop! For God's sake, stop it!

RIBADIER collapses on the sofa, his head in his hands.

ANGÈLE: (*getting up*) Well, it's not my fault. You cast the spell on me!

RIBADIER: So what? You should have called out! You should have screamed!

ANGÈLE: Screamed! But one only screams in nightmares. And I couldn't honestly say this was a nightmare…

RIBADIER: (*leaping up*) Oh! That's quite enough, Madame!

ANGÈLE: I *could* say, in my unconscious state, I thought it was you…

RIBADIER: Me! Hardly! All those evenings! When I'd already… Come along!

ANGÈLE: Oh, I know it wasn't you. I mean I know what you're like…only too well! A man is sparing at home when he is lavish abroad.

RIBADIER: Oh! Oh!

ANGÈLE: It's all right. I understand… A minister can't serve both the Home Office and the Foreign Office at the same time.

RIBADIER: Oh! That's enough!

ANGÈLE: The terrible truth is that this is all your own fault.

RIBADIER: Yes, you're right! Oh, please, please go… I want to be alone. I need a moment to think…

ANGÈLE: Eugène, you left me defenceless. Something like this was inevitable.

ANGÈLE makes for her bedroom.

RIBADIER: Oh, I'll find the degenerate bastard!

ANGÈLE: (*aside*) Good luck! You'll need it!

ANGÈLE exits.

Scene 6

RIBADIER: (*alone; very agitated*) Oh, it's dreadful! Quite appalling! And it's all my own doing, idiot that I am! Other men content themselves with traditional techniques to deceive their wives… I had to be too clever by half! My own unique system! The Ribadier Method! (*collapsing on the pouf*) And look where it's got me! Right by the b –

THOMMEREUX burts in.

THOMMEREUX: – I went to your President's place. He can't do it; he's dead. That effectively rules him out.

RIBADIER: (*getting up*) Oh, the duel… I've more pressing things to think about…

THOMMEREUX: Really?

RIBADIER: You know that dream my wife had? The one she wouldn't tell me in front of you…

THOMMEREUX: (*aside*) Oh, dear!

RIBADIER: Well, now she has revealed all.

THOMMEREUX: (*very embarrassed*) Really? She's come out with… (*aside*) Oh, my God!

RIBADIER: Listen to this! While I was out with Madame Savinet, apparently, some vile degenerate was making his way in here!

THOMMEREUX: (*aside*) Oh, la, la, la, la, la!

RIBADIER: Every single time, my friend.

THOMMEREUX: No. Not every time.

RIBADIER: Oh, yes! Each and every time.

THOMMEREUX: But that wasn't me!

RIBADIER: I know perfectly well it wasn't you. D'you think I told you because I suspected you?

THOMMEREUX: No!… No. I was just thinking… But what is it you're saying?… Some intruder's been in here?

RIBADIER: (*nodding*) And taken the most despicable advantage of Angèle's state to –

THOMMEREUX: – don't! Don't finish! Don't say it! I don't want to know…

RIBADIER: Then you do already!

THOMMEREUX: Angèle…your wife… Madame Ribadier…all those evenings!

THOMMEREUX falls on the sofa. RIBADIER slumps onto the pouf.

RIBADIER: Yes!

A pause as they contemplate the full horror of the discovery.

THOMMEREUX: And you just blurt it out like this! To me! Have you no discretion?

RIBADIER: I've only just heard. You can see what a state I'm in!

THOMMEREUX: You're in a state! What about the rest of us?… Anyway, why are *you* so concerned? You don't love her!

RIBADIER: I do!… I certainly can't bear the thought of her with anyone else!

THOMMEREUX: Ah!… Who is he, this foul pervert?

RIBADIER: (*getting up*) An unknown.

THOMMEREUX: (*getting up forcefully*) What's his name?

RIBADIER: He's an unknown!

THOMMEREUX: That's terrific! An unknown! We don't know who he is! Don't you suspect anyone?

RIBADIER: Ah! No-one and everyone!

THOMMEREUX: Everyone? The whole world is Angèle's lover! That's just dandy! Three cheers for the Ribadier Method! Bravo!

RIBADIER: Oh, the swine! The bastard! To think he got in each night through this window.

RIBADIER goes to the French windows.

THOMMEREUX: It's disgusting!

RIBADIER: (*a sharp yelp*) Oh! Something's caught here. A clue!

THOMMEREUX: Eh?

RIBADIER: A button. A trouser button… With a scrap of material still attached…

THOMMEREUX: A button…

Feverishly, he checks his own trousers.

(*aside*) No. Thank God! Not mine.

RIBADIER: (*moving downstage*) It's yellow.

THOMMEREUX: Cruel irony!

RIBADIER: Whose is it? Who?… A trouser button… All men wear trousers; that tells us nothing.

THOMMEREUX: Well, it tells us it's a man!

RIBADIER: Brilliant! That narrows it down to half the human race.

THOMMEREUX: (*overcome*) One woman…and half the human race!

RIBADIER: Oh, it's enough to drive one mad!

Scene 7

SOPHIE enters.

SOPHIE: Monsieur, Gusman's here.

RIBADIER: Go to hell, both of you!

SOPHIE: Eh?

GUSMAN: (*entering*) It's me, Monsieur. I just came to get my orders for the day.

RIBADIER: There are no orders. Be off!

THOMMEREUX: There are no orders. Be off!

GUSMAN: (*aside*) What's he got to do with it?

> *GUSMAN turns away revealing the unbuttoned flap of his trousers with their missing button.*

RIBADIER: (*another yelp*) Ah!

ALL: What?

RIBADIER: Look at his button! It's not there!

THOMMEREUX: Eh?

GUSMAN: (*to SOPHIE*) What's up with them?

THOMMEREUX: The coachman!

> *RIBADIER hurls himself at GUSMAN's throat and drags him downstage. THOMMEREUX follows suit.*

RIBADIER: Oh, you wretch!

THOMMEREUX: Oh, you fiend!

GUSMAN: Oh, my God!

RIBADIER / THOMMEREUX: (*shaking him*) Oh, it's you! It's you!!

GUSMAN: Well, yes, it's me!

> *RIBADIER releases GUSMAN and turns to THOMMEREUX.*

RIBADIER: (*coldly*) I'm going to strangle him.

GUSMAN / SOPHIE: What??

RIBADIER: (*to SOPHIE*) Leave us.

GUSMAN / SOPHIE: Yes, Monsieur.

RIBADIER: (*to GUSMAN*) *You* are staying! (*to SOPHIE*) I was talking to you. Off you go.

SOPHIE: Yes, Monsieur. (*aside*) What are they going to do to him? My God!

SOPHIE exits. THOMMEREUX forces GUSMAN to sit down on the pouf.

RIBADIER: To think that this is the man who seduced my… And here he is! Right in front of me!

THOMMEREUX: Large as life!

GUSMAN: (*aside*) Why are they staring at me like that?

Self-conscious under their scrutiny, GUSMAN smiles.

RIBADIER: Look at him!… He's smiling… He has the audacity to smile… I'm going to kill him!

GUSMAN leaps up and moves out of the way.

GUSMAN: Hey, hey, hey!

THOMMEREUX: (*restraining RIBADIER*) Not yet!… First, we must know everything!… Grill him…but be subtle!

RIBADIER: Right.

THOMMEREUX: Be diplomatic! Let me do it! I have the experience… I was Consul out in Saigon.

RIBADIER: Go on.

THOMMEREUX: (*sitting on the pouf*) Step forward, young man!

GUSMAN approaches fearfully.

Right! Coachman! Are you or are you not the vile seducer of –

RIBADIER: (*stopping him*) Hey! Shut up, for God's sake!

RIBADIER pushes THOMMEREUX off the pouf.

If that's your diplomacy, I fear for the Republic!

THOMMEREUX: What? It was going so well! I had him –

RIBADIER: (*sitting on the pouf*) – Be quiet! Right. Let me do it. (*to GUSMAN*) Come here! Do you recognize this?

GUSMAN: It's the button from my trousers.

RIBADIER: (*getting up, trimphantly*) His button! He said so himself! It's his button!

GUSMAN: Well, yes! I've been looking for it.

RIBADIER grabs him by the collar.

RIBADIER: It's your button, you scoundrel!

GUSMAN: Yes!… Shall I take it now?

RIBADIER: It was you, was it not, who climbed in here every night I was out?

GUSMAN: Monsieur knows!

RIBADIER: Everything!

THOMMEREUX: Everything!

RIBADIER: You came for a woman, didn't you? Come on now, confess it!

GUSMAN: Oh, Monsieur!… Gallantry doesn't permit me to… I'm a gentleman!

RIBADIER: (*holding his anger in check*) Ouf!… Come along, come along! There's fifty francs in it for you…

GUSMAN: (*with dignity*) Agreed!

RIBADIER: S o, it is you who's been climbing up here in the dark.

GUSMAN: It was me!

RIBADIER: And you took care never to turn up the lamp!

GUSMAN: You bet! And I crept about on tip-toes!

RIBADIER / THOMMEREUX: Oh!

RIBADIER: And you dared… You dared to take your pleasure with this poor innocent creature, against her will?

GUSMAN: What?

RIBADIER: You forced yourself upon her!

GUSMAN: No! Now, really… She was the one who came on to me!

RIBADIER / THOMMEREUX: Eh?

RIBADIER: Dishonour!

THOMMEREUX: Oh, Angèle!

GUSMAN: (*aside*) What a fuss over a maid!

RIBADIER: (*in despair*) It was she who made advances to you?

GUSMAN: She's always had a weakness for the stables!

THOMMEREUX: Oh!

RIBADIER: Oh, stop! Stop! (*aside*) Jezebel! (*aloud*) Right! In there! Off you go! And don't come out till I tell you. All right?

RIBADIER shoves GUSMAN in the direction of the dining room.

GUSMAN: And my fifty francs, Monsieur?

RIBADIER: Your fifty francs! You ask me… He'll want a tip next!

THOMMEREUX: Shameless!

RIBADIER: Get in there! Now!

Scene 8

RIBADIER collapses in THOMMEREUX's arms.

RIBADIER: Oh, my friend. My dear fellow! It's too awful!

THOMMEREUX: It's monstrous!

RIBADIER: Oh, the little hypocrite! Who'd ever suspect her when she was so suspicious herself?

THOMMEREUX: Eh?

RIBADIER: And whom does she choose, eh? Her coachman! Not even a man of substance…

THOMMEREUX: And when she's offered a man of substance, she doesn't want him!

RIBADIER: But a coachman! A servant!

THOMMEREUX: Oh, my poor friend, that's a bitter pill to swallow…

RIBADIER marches over to ANGÈLE's bedroom door.

RIBADIER: Oh, just you wait, Madame! (*calling*) Angèle! Angèle! (*returning to THOMMEREUX*) No, I mean, I'm a man of the world. I take most things in my stride… But this!!… No. No!

ANGÈLE enters from her bedroom.

ANGÈLE: Did you call?

RIBADIER: Approach, Madame. I know everything!

THOMMEREUX: We know everything, Madame!

ANGÈLE: What, precisely?

RIBADIER: What took place in this very room… The unknown man, here, every night… In through the window!

ANGÈLE: Well, I told you that!

RIBADIER: Yes, but you didn't tell me that you knew him, this mysterious intruder… And now we know who he is too!

ANGÈLE: Oh, really?

RIBADIER / THOMMEREUX: Absolutely!

ANGÈLE: You've found him out! Congratulations! (*aside*) They really fell for it…

RIBADIER: And he has told us everything, Madame! Everything, you understand!…

ANGÈLE: Ah!?!

THOMMEREUX: Everything!

RIBADIER: And it wasn't him who took advantage of you! It was you who went after him!

ANGÈLE: Eh?

RIBADIER: Oh, the shame of it! He's in there, your lover! Yes, Madame, your lover is right next door!

ANGÈLE: In there?

RIBADIER marches over to the dining room door.

RIBADIER: In here! May I present your lover! (*opening the door*) Come out!

GUSMAN appears.

THOMMEREUX: Come out!

ANGÈLE: The coachman!

RIBADIER: He's told all. Confessed everything!

ANGÈLE: What? You!

GUSMAN: Yes, Madame, I've confessed everything. I confess it again before you.

ANGÈLE: But it's all lies!

GUSMAN: What do you mean?

ANGÈLE: (*going to RIBADIER*) You don't believe him, do you? I couldn't bear it if you believed him!

RIBADIER / THOMMEREUX: Eh?

ANGÈLE: Never! Never, ever, ever! I swear it!…

ANGÈLE lowers her voice so that GUSMAN cannot hear.

The whole thing was an invention. I made it up because I wanted to make you suffer just a fraction of what you've made me suffer! Now, I've no idea what's going on here, but you can't seriously imagine that I would…. No! It's not true. Me! With your coachman. Never, never, never!

RIBADIER: But what can all this mean? (*to GUSMAN*) Ah! You! Where are you going!… Who was the woman with –

GUSMAN: – Sophie, Monsieur! The maid.

RIBADIER / THOMMEREUX: Sophie!

ANGÈLE: Ah! I knew it!

GUSMAN: (*looking round*) Who else could it be?

In spite of herself, ANGÈLE is a little piqued.

RIBADIER: Nobody! (*aside; in transports of delight*) It was Sophie! (*aloud*) Gusman! I owe you fifty francs. Here's twenty. You'll get the rest!

GUSMAN: Eh? But, Monsieur, that wasn't the deal.

RIBADIER: It is now. I won't discuss it further.

GUSMAN: Oh, that's not fair! (*aside*) Never mind! I'll make it back on the oats.

Scene 9

RIBADIER: Oh, Angèle, it was very naughty of you to play with me like that…

RIBADIER goes to embrace ANGÈLE.

ANGÈLE turns away from him.

You do still love me, don't you?

ANGÈLE: My only regret, Monsieur, is that you didn't suffer more and for longer… It's all over between us!

RIBADIER: (*perturbed*) No! No! Nothing's over. You still love me!

ANGÈLE: No, I'm not sure I do.

THOMMEREUX: (*suddenly hopeful*) Ah ha!

THOMMEREUX takes up a protective position by ANGÈLE. He watches their tennis match exchange like an avid fan.

RIBADIER: You want your freedom?

ANGÈLE: Well, you clearly want yours!

RIBADIER: Oh, Angèle! What? You mean to cast me back into the arms of Madame Savinet.

ANGÈLE: (*scornfully*) Réré!!

A beat. ANGÈLE is torn: she is still angry but cannot bear the thought of RIBADIER with another woman.

You wouldn't go back to her, would you?

RIBADIER: Well…? I don't *want* to… Angèle, I want to give up my post in the Foreign Office and devote myself to Domestic Affairs from now on…

ANGÈLE: (*melting*) Oh, Eugène!…

ANGÈLE and RIBADIER appear about to embrace.

THOMMEREUX: (*hastily*) But can you trust him? The man's a pathological liar! He's a politician!

RIBADIER: Hey!

ANGÈLE freezes and looks at RIBADIER doubtfully.

THOMMEREUX: Mind you, there's the duel, of course. (*smugly*) Death should ensure fidelity…

RIBADIER claps his hand to his forehead. He'd forgotten the duel. ANGÈLE smiles, realising that SAVINET has given her the upper hand in this relationship.

RIBADIER: Oh, my God! My God!

A beat. ANGÈLE, relishing his fear, waits before intervening.

ANGÈLE: Actually, Monsieur Savinet is prepared to 'suspend' his challenge –

RIBADIER / THOMMEREUX: Eh?!?

ANGÈLE: Yes. So long as I keep the secret of your adultery with his wife.

RIBADIER / THOMMEREUX: Ah!

RIBADIER takes ANGÈLE in his arms.

RIBADIER: I'll give you no reason to tell, that I promise you!

ANGÈLE: See you don't.

RIBADIER and ANGÈLE embrace.

THOMMEREUX: Oh, really! That's it, I suppose! Well, there's nothing left for me… Right. I shall kill myself!

THOMMEREUX marches determinedly towards the balcony. As he unfastens the French windows, he glances back at

RIBADIER and ANGÈLE who, locked in an embrace, have taken no notice of his dramatic announcement.

(*loudly*) I'm about to hurl myself off the balcony!

No reaction.

RIBADIER: I only have one…'request'. (*pointing at the portrait*) That we get rid of that painting…

ANGÈLE is about to protest.

(*gently silences her*) …And replace it with a new portrait of you.

THOMMEREUX has thrown one leg over the balustrade.

THOMMEREUX: I'M GOING…

Still no reaction.

ANGÈLE: (*musing*) Another Manet?…

THOMMEREUX: He's DEAD!… Not that you two would care!

ANGÈLE: Hmmm… No. Renoir for me, I think.

RIBADIER: Perfect.

ANGÈLE and RIBADIER embrace again.

THOMMEREUX: Ouf!… Not again. Well, really… Some people! (*climbing back inside*) Still, there's no point with (*indicating the portrait*) only him watching… Hah! Thommereux, old fellow! It's time to go: Eastward ho!

The End.